THE COMPREHENSIVE

WOOD PELLET GRILL

COOKBOOK

1000-DAY TASTY AND DELICIOUS WOOD PELLET GRILL RECIPES FOR BEGINNERS

NICK OGLESBY

CONTENTS

INTRODUCTION

What Exactly Are Wood Pellets?

Wood pellets are made from a combination of hardwood shavings and sawdust. This is pressurized, compressed down, and held together through the use of the wood's lignin, an all-natural binding agent. It's made into long, pencil-thick rods that are broken into smaller pieces. Most wood pellet pieces will be about a half-inch long.

During the compression of the wood shaving and sawdust mixture, most of the air and moisture is removed. Also, this mixture means you won't be burning any bark, dirt, etc that you would find on raw wood logs. This results in an extremely efficient and clean-burning fuel source. Pellets used for smoking are also food-grade. Therefore, they do not contain any adhesives or chemicals. They also don't contain softwoods, like pine or spruce, that have a high amount of sap that can adversely affect the taste of your meat.

Most wood pellets are made up of mainly oak, a very stable burning wood. This is then blended with another hardwood or fruitwood to impart the flavor through the smoke.

The Operation Principle of Weber Wood Pellet Grill

Wood pellet grills use an auger that moves the hardwood pellets from the hopper to the fire pot underneath the grill. The higher the set temperature, the more pellets are dispensed into the auger. Once in the fire pot, a hot rod ignites the pellets creating a fire, then a fan stokes the fire creating convection heat to evenly cook your food in the grill. A drip tray sits over the fire pot, keeping the direct flames off your food while catching food drippings to help prevent flare-ups.

The Advantages of Your Weber Wood Pellet Grill

1. The Weber wood pellet grill makes barbecuing easy.

Plug it in, fill the hopper with BBQ pellets, turn it on, set the temperature, and let the grill do the rest. Pellet grills are designed to allow one to take a hands-off approach to cooking by letting a controller do the majority of the work.

You don't need to haul logs or arrange charcoal. You can put away the lighter fluid and flint. The Ignition sequence on a pellet grill starts with a single button press.

Once the ignition sequence is complete, the controller's capabilities determine to what extent it is able to control the cooking process. Pellet grill controllers have evolved over time from simple low, medium, & high setting devices to the advanced controllers found on high end pellet grills today.

The programs and algorithms that comprise its firmware were designed by us to ensure peak performance, consistency, and accuracy whether you're grilling steaks in the sub-zero Alaskan winter or smoking a brisket all day in the blistering deserts of Arizona.

This level of control also allows you to choose cook length, temperature, and when that temperature should change. You're in control and can fully customize the longest and most complicated of cooks to your exact specifications.

Add to this the convenience of technologies like Wi-Fi and BlueTooth and it's easy to see the appeal of the work smarter, not harder approach to smoking and grilling meat.

2. The Weber wood pellet grill is safe.

Gas can explode. Charcoal and wood logs are messy and can smolder for days after use. Direct cooking over fire increases the likelihood of flare ups and grease fires.

Pellet grills cook indirectly, meaning no open flame, flying sparks, or direct contact between fat drippings and fire. MAK Pellet grills create small, precisely controlled fires in a stainless-steel firepot. This firepot is surrounded by a stainless-steel body and covered by a stainless-steel diffuser, and drip pan at a minimum.

Pellets are released in small quantities and consumed completely. As long as you maintain relatively minimal cleaning routines, which we make as easy as possible by using a removable firepot, the chances of anything out of the ordinary happening are extremely low.

The pellet grill is the safest outdoor cooking device ever invented.

3.Pellet grilling is better for your health and the environment. No added oils or fats are needed to achieve the tremendous flavor that cooking on a pellet grill imparts. You're cooking with real wood, which means you're using a fuel that has been used since the dawn of time. Because you are cooking indirectly, excess animal fat drippings are not burned up and made carcinogenic by open flame. Instead, they hit a grease pan and convert to gases which help flavor your food. Hardwood BBQ pellets burn with a more than 98% efficiency. This reduces the exposure of carcinogenic substances and HCA's to you and the environment. Avoiding the creation of carcinogenic smoke is not only good for your health. Extremely low particulate matter means fresher, safer air to breathe. Barbecue pellets reduce landfill disposal of sawdust by millions of tons per year. Barbecue pellets are not only a sustainable biofuel, they are also the ultimate example of re-purposing.

Tips for Using Your Weber Wood Pellet Grill

1. Season your new pellet grill.

Season your new pellet grill according to the manufacturer's directions (a process that usually takes 45 minutes to one hour). This burns off any residual oils from the manufacturing process.

2. Allow yourself some time to get acquainted with your new grill/smoker.

Allow yourself some time to get acquainted with your new grill/smoker. We know you'll be anxious to try it out, but don't be overly ambitious. Instead of a whole brisket, which could take 15 hours or more, or a budget-busting prime rib roast, start with chicken (parts, such as breasts or wings, or a whole bird), pork loin tenderloin, or blade (shoulder) steaks, Cornish hens, salmon steaks or fillets, or other relatively inexpensive cuts that can be completed in 2 hours or less.

3. Identify any hot spots—most grills have them.

Identify any hot spots—most grills have them. Preheat your grill to medium-high as directed by the owner's manual, then lay slices of cheap white bread shoulder to shoulder across the grate. Watch carefully, then flip after a few minutes. Take a photo of the results. The darkest bread will indicate where the temperature might be hotter. (Print the photo out and add it to your owner's manual for reference.)

4. Don't let your meat come to room temperature before cooking.

Whatever meat you select, put it on the preheated grill/smoker straight from the refrigerator. Do not, as many recipes suggest, allow it to come to room temperature before cooking.

As Steven often notes, high-end steak houses do not leave their meats out at room temperature. (The danger area is 40 to 140 degrees.) The heat of the grill is sufficient to raise the internal temperature of the meat by those few degrees.

5. Invest in a good meat thermometer.

A laser-type thermometer such as this one will give you a more accurate temperature reading at grill level than a built-in dome thermometer. Determine the temperature range of your grill model from lowest to highest (180 degrees to 500+, for example).

Cleaning Your Weber Wood Pellet Grill

For spot-cleaning the outside of your grill, you can simply use a dry cloth to remove grease marks, dust and dirt quickly. To perform a deep clean, use a soft cloth with soap and water, stainless steel cleaner or a bbq degreaser. Follow these steps to clean the outside of your BBQ:

1. Make sure your grill is cold before spraying any cleaner on the outside of your grill.
2. Apply your cleaner using a soft cloth or spray bottle. If spraying cleaner onto your pellet grill, be very careful not to get any inside of your grill. Avoid spraying stainless steel cleaner onto plastic components as it can cause them to degrade more quickly.
3. Allow the cleaner to sit for at least 30 seconds to break down any dried grease or food residue.
4. Wipe the cleaner off with a clean cloth or paper towel. If cleaning a stainless steel BBQ, wipe in the same direction as the grain. If your smoker has a painted surface, wipe in circles.
5. Repeat this process as necessary until all of the dirt and grime is removed.
6. Using a wet cloth, wipe down the surface of the grill to remove all remaining cleaner or soap residue. Do not rinse your pellet grill with a hose or bucket as water can get into the grill or hopper and cause damage its electrical components or ruin the pellets.

Always unplug your pellet grill from its power source before cleaning it with water or liquid cleaner and allow it to dry for at least 24 hours before your next grilling session. Empty your wood pellets from the hopper before cleaning and check that there is no water or cleaner in the hopper before putting the pellets back in.

SEAFOOD RECIPES

Honey Balsamic Salmon

Servings: 2

Cooking Time: 25 Minutes

Ingredients:

- 1 Medium salmon fillet
- Fin & Feather Rub
- 1/2 Cup balsamic vinegar
- 1 Tablespoon minced garlic
- 2 Tablespoon honey

Directions:

1. Season the fillet with the Traeger Fin & Feather Rub.
2. Make the glaze: Combine the vinegar, garlic and honey in a small saucepan. Simmer over medium heat until reduced by half. Usually 10 to 15 minutes. The glaze will be properly reduced when it coats the back of a spoon. Using a basting brush, coat the fillet with the glaze.
3. Supply your smoker with wood pellets and follow the start-up procedure. Preheat the grill, with the lid closed, to 350° F.
4. Arrange the salmon fillet on the grill grate. Grill for 25 to 30 minutes, or until the salmon is opaque and flakes easily with a fork. Grill: 350 ˚F
5. Transfer to a platter or plates and serve immediately. If desired, heat any remaining glaze to a boil and drizzle over top of the salmon. Enjoy!

Whole Vermillion Red Snapper

Servings: 6

Cooking Time: 20 Minutes

Ingredients:

➢ 1 Whole Vermillion Red Snapper, scaled & gutted

➢ 4 Clove garlic, chopped

➢ 1 Whole lemon, thinly sliced

➢ 2 Sprig rosemary sprigs

➢ sea salt and freshly ground black pepper

Directions:

1. Supply your smoker with wood pellets and follow the start-up procedure. Preheat the grill, with the lid closed, to High heat.

2. Stuff the cavity of the fish with chopped garlic. Sprinkle the fish with sea salt, pepper, rosemary, and lemon.

3. Grill fish directly on the grill grate. Cook for 20-25 minutes. Serve. Enjoy!

Mezcal Shrimp With Salsa De Molcajete

Servings: 4   Cooking Time: 14 Minutes

Ingredients:

- 18 to 24 jumbo shrimp, about 1½lb (680g) total, peeled and deveined
- ⅓ cup mezcal
- juice of ½ lime
- 2 tbsp extra virgin olive oil
- 2 tsp coarse salt
- 1 tsp ground cumin
- lime wedges
- for the salsa
- 2 Roma tomatoes
- 2 tomatillos, husked and washed
- 2 garlic cloves, peeled and impaled on a toothpick
- 1 jalapeño or serrano pepper
- 1 small white onion, halved
- ½ tsp coarse salt, plus more
- juice of ½ lime
- ¼ cup loosely packed fresh cilantro leaves

Directions:

1. Supply your smoker with wood pellets and follow the start-up procedure. Preheat the grill, with the lid closed, to 450° F.

2. In a large bowl, combine the shrimp, mezcal, lime juice, olive oil, salt, and ground cumin. Toss with your hands to mix thoroughly. Set aside for 15 minutes and then toss once more.

3. Begin to make the salsa by placing the tomatoes, tomatillos, garlic, jalapeño, and onion on the grate. Grill until they begin to char, about 3 minutes for the garlic and about 6 to 8 minutes for the other vegetables, turning as needed. Transfer the vegetables to a rimmed sheet pan. Remove the skewers from the garlic. Let everything cool. Coarsely chop the vegetables and leave them in separate piles.

4. Place the garlic in the molcajete and add the salt. Mash the garlic to a purée using the temolote. Add the onion and grind it into the garlic paste. Stir in the jalapeño (deseeded for a milder salsa), tomatoes, and tomatillos. Stir in the lime juice and cilantro leaves. Taste, adding salt. (If you don't own a molcajete or temolote, prepare the salsa using a small food processor.)

5. Drain the shrimp and discard the marinade. Thread the shrimp on wood or bamboo skewers. Place the shrimp on the grate and grill until they're white and opaque, about 4 to 6 minutes, tossing with tongs.

6. Transfer the shrimp to a platter. Serve with the salsa and lime wedges.

Seared Bluefin Tuna Steaks

Servings: 2

Cooking Time: 5 Minutes

Ingredients:

- 3 Whole Tuna, steak
- olive oil
- salt and pepper
- soy sauce
- Sriracha

Directions:

1. Lightly baste both sides of tuna steaks in olive oil; sprinkle sea salt and ground pepper on each side.

2. Supply your smoker with wood pellets and follow the start-up procedure. Preheat the grill, with the lid closed, to High heat.

3. Grill tuna steaks on each side for 2 to 2-1/2 minutes.

4. Remove tuna from grill and allow to cool slightly.

5. Cut into 1/2 - 3/4" pieces. Serve with a mixture of Soy Sauce and Sriracha. Enjoy!"

Grilled Maple Syrup Salmon

Servings: 6

Cooking Time: 30 Minutes

Ingredients:

- ➢ 1 large salmon fillet (around 3 pounds)
- ➢ 1/2 cup salted butter (melted)
- ➢ 2 tablespoons soy sauce
- ➢ Salt and pepper
- ➢ 1/4 cup maple syrup

Directions:

1. Supply your smoker with wood pellets and follow the start-up procedure. Preheat the grill, with the lid closed, to 400° F.
2. Place the salmon fillet in a baking pan lined with parchment paper.
3. Sprinkle the fish with salt and pepper.
4. Add half of the melted butter to the salmon and place the baking pan on the grill.
5. Grill for 15-20 minutes or until fish is roughly 70% cooked. It will feel still gelatinous in the thickest parts of the salmon.
6. Combine the remaining melted butter, soy sauce, and maple syrup and pour over the salmon.It will run off the sides so use a spoon to pour it back over the fish. It's also perfectly fine that some will be left on the sides of the pan.
7. Cook for 5 to 10 additional minutes or until the fish is cooked through. The fish should be firm to the touch but still moist and soft when pressed on,and the ridges will flake or pull apart if pressed on.

Smoked Salt Cured Lox

Servings: 8

Cooking Time: 30 Minutes

Ingredients:

- ➤ 1 Cup kosher salt
- ➤ 1 Cup sugar
- ➤ 1 Tablespoon cracked black pepper
- ➤ 1 Whole lemon zest
- ➤ 1 Whole orange zest
- ➤ 1 Whole Packaged Dill, roughly chopped including stems
- ➤ 2 Pound salmon fillet, skin on

Directions:

1. Mix together salt, sugar, black pepper, lemon zest, orange zest, and dill.

2. Slice salmon in half. Coat all flesh of salmon completely with salt sugar mixture. Sandwich the 2 pieces together, flesh to flesh and completely cover with salt sugar mixture.

3. Wrap tightly with plastic wrap and place into a gallon zip top bag. Squeeze out as much air as possible. Place wrapped salmon into a baking dish and place something heavy on top like a pot filled with water or a brick wrapped in foil. Place into the refrigerator for 10 hours. After 10 hours, flip over and put the weight back on top. Refrigerate for another 10 hours.

4. Remove from refrigerator, unwrap and rinse of remaining salt with cold water. Pat dry and leave on counter for 1 hour.

5. Supply your smoker with wood pellets and follow the start-up procedure. Preheat the grill, with the lid closed, to 180° F.

6. Place salmon onto a baking pan. Fill another baking pan with ice and place baking pan with salmon over ice.

7. Place onto grill and smoke for 30 minutes. Remove from grill and slice thin. Grill: 180 °F

8. Serve with bagels, cream cheese, capers, dill, lemon wedges, sliced tomatoes, and red onion. Enjoy!

Smoked Fish Chowder

Servings: 4

Cooking Time: 60 Minutes

Ingredients:

- ➢ 12 Ounce (1-1/2 to 2 lb) skin-on salmon fillet, preferably wild-caught
- ➢ Fin & Feather Rub
- ➢ 2 Corn Husks
- ➢ 3 Slices Bacon, sliced
- ➢ 4 Can Cream of Potato Soup, Condensed
- ➢ 3 Cup whole milk
- ➢ 8 Ounce cream cheese
- ➢ 3 green onions, thinly sliced
- ➢ 2 Teaspoon hot sauce

Directions:

1. Supply your smoker with wood pellets and follow the start-up procedure. Preheat the grill, with the lid closed, to 180° F.

2. Sprinkle Traeger Fin & Feather rub as needed on salmon. Arrange the salmon skin-side down on the grill grate. Smoke for 30 minutes. Grill: 180 ˚F

3. Increase the grill temperature to 350˚F. Grill: 350 ˚F

4. Cook the salmon for 30 minutes, or until the fish flakes easily with a fork. (The exact time will depend on the thickness of the fillet.) There is no need to turn the fish. Using a large thin spatula, transfer the salmon to a wire rack to cool. Remove the skin. (The salmon can be made a day ahead, wrapped in plastic wrap and refrigerated.) Break into flakes and set aside.

5. Arrange the corn and bacon strips on the grill grate. (The salmon will be roasting while you do this.) Roast the corn and the bacon until the corn is cooked through and browned in spots, turning as needed, and the bacon is crisp, about 15 minutes.

6. In the meantime, bring the cream of potato soup and the milk to a simmer over medium heat in a large saucepan or Dutch oven on the stovetop. Gradually stir in the cream cheese and whisk to blend. Chop the bacon into bits and slice the corn off the cobs using long strokes of a chef's knife.

7. Add to the soup along with the green onions. Stir in the salmon. Heat gently for 5 to 10 minutes. Add the hot sauce to taste. If the chowder is too thick, add more milk. Serve at once. Enjoy!

Bbq Roasted Salmon

Servings: 4

Cooking Time: 15 Minutes

Ingredients:

- ➢ 1/3 Cup honey
- ➢ 3 Tablespoon Mustard, whole-grain
- ➢ 1 Cup ketchup
- ➢ 1/2 Cup dark brown sugar
- ➢ 1 Teaspoon Cider Vinegar
- ➢ 1/2 Teaspoon Thyme Leaves, finely chopped
- ➢ 1/8 Teaspoon Jacobsen Salt Co. Pure Kosher Sea Salt
- ➢ 1/8 Teaspoon freshly ground black pepper
- ➢ 4 Whole Salmon Fillets, 6oz each, skin-on

Directions:

1. Combine all sauce ingredients in a large bowl, preferably one day prior to making the salmon.
2. Rub salmon fillets on both sides with sauce. Reserve any extra, unused sauce.
3. Supply your smoker with wood pellets and follow the start-up procedure. Preheat the grill, with the lid closed, to 350° F.
4. Place fillets on grill, skin-side down, and cook for 15 minutes. Grill: 350 ˚F
5. Let the fish rest for about 3-5 minutes. Serve with extra sauce. Enjoy!

Lemon Shrimp Scampi

Servings: 3

Cooking Time: 10 Minutes

Ingredients:

- 2 Tsp Blackened Sriracha Rub Seasoning
- 1/2 Cup Butter, Cubed, Divided
- 1/2 Tsp Chili Pepper Flakes
- 3 Garlic Cloves, Minced
- To Taste, Lemon Wedges, For Serving
- 1 Lemon, Juice & Zest
- Linguine, Cooked
- 3 Tbsp Parsley, Chopped
- 1 1/2 Lbs Shrimp, Peeled & Deveined
- Toasted Baguette, For Serving

Directions:

1. Supply your smoker with wood pellets and follow the start-up procedure. Preheat the grill, with the lid closed, to medium-high heat. If using a gas or charcoal grill, set it up for medium-high heat.
2. Add half of the butter to the griddle, then sauté the garlic, Blackened Sriracha, and chili flakes for 1 minute, until fragrant.
3. Add the shrimp, turning occasionally for 2 minutes, until opaque.
4. Add the remaining butter, parsley, lemon zest and juice. Toss the shrimp to coat in lemon butter, then remove from the griddle, and transfer to a serving bowl.
5. Serve immediately, with fresh lemon wedges, and toasted baguette. Serve over linguine, spaghetti or zucchini noodles, if desired.

Lobster Tail

Servings: 2

Cooking Time: 25 Minutes

Ingredients:

- ➢ 2 lobster tails
- ➢ Salt
- ➢ Freshly ground black pepper
- ➢ 1 batch Lemon Butter Mop for Seafood

Directions:

1. Supply your smoker with wood pellets and follow the start-up procedure. Preheat the grill, with the lid closed, to 375°F.

2. Using kitchen shears, slit the top of the lobster shells, through the center, nearly to the tail. Once cut, expose as much meat as you can through the cut shell.

3. Season the lobster tails all over with salt and pepper.

4. Place the tails directly on the grill grate and grill until their internal temperature reaches 145°F. Remove the lobster from the grill and serve with the mop on the side for dipping.

Traeger Jerk Shrimp

Servings: 8

Cooking Time: 10 Minutes

Ingredients:

- 1 Tablespoon brown sugar
- 1 Tablespoon smoked paprika
- 1 Teaspoon garlic powder
- 1/4 Teaspoon Thyme, ground
- 1/4 Teaspoon ground cayenne pepper
- 1 Teaspoon sea salt
- 1 lime zest
- 2 Pound shrimp in shell
- 3 Tablespoon olive oil

Directions:

1. Combine spices, salt, and lime zest in a small bowl and mix. Place shrimp into a large bowl, then drizzle in the olive oil, Add the spice mixture and toss to combine, making sure every shrimp is kissed with deliciousness.

2. Supply your smoker with wood pellets and follow the start-up procedure. Preheat the grill, with the lid closed, to 450° F.

3. Arrange the shrimp on the grill and cook for 2 – 3 minutes per side, until firm, opaque, and cooked through. Grill: 450 ℉

4. Serve with lime wedges, fresh cilantro, mint, and Caribbean Hot Pepper Sauce. Enjoy!

BAKING RECIPES

Eggs Ham Benedict

Servings: 6

Cooking Time: 15 Minutes

Ingredients:

- ➢ 1 Biscuit Dough, Tube
- ➢ 6 Egg
- ➢ 16 Ham, Sliced
- ➢ 1 Packet Hollandaise Sauce, Package

Directions:

1. Supply your smoker with wood pellets and follow the start-up procedure. Preheat the grill, with the lid closed, to 350° F.

2. Grease a muffin tin and crack an egg in each cup. Place on the grate of the for about 10 minutes or until the whites are fully cooked.

3. At the same time, place your biscuit dough on a greased pan. Follow the directions on the packaging but bake on the . Place 2 slices of ham per biscuit on the pan as well.

4. While the ham, eggs, and biscuits are cooking, prepare the Hollandaise Sauce according to the directions on the packet.

5. When everything is fully cooked, cut a biscuit in half, and stack one or two slices of ham, 1 egg and a dollop of Hollandaise sauce. Repeat for each half biscuit. Serve with fresh fruit.

Baked Irish Creme Cake

Servings: 4

Cooking Time: 60 Minutes

Ingredients:

- 1 Cup Pecans, pieces
- 1 Yellow Cake Mix, Boxed
- 1 Vanilla Pudding Mix, Instant Package (3.4oz)
- 4 Large eggs
- 1/2 Cup water
- 1/2 Cup vegetable oil
- 1 Cup Irish Cream Liquor
- 1/2 Cup butter
- 1 Cup sugar

Directions:

1. Grease and flour a 10" (25 cm) Bundt pan. Sprinkle pecans along the bottom.

2. In a large bowl, with a mixer, combine yellow cake mix, pudding mix, eggs, water, oil, and Irish Cream liquor. Pour batter over nuts in the pan.

3. Supply your smoker with wood pellets and follow the start-up procedure. Preheat the grill, with the lid closed, to 325° F.

4. Place Bundt pan on the Traeger and bake for 1 hour, or until a toothpick comes out clean. Remove from heat, cool for 10 minutes. Grill: 325 °F

5. While the cake is cooling, combine the butter, water and sugar and bring to a boil. Boil for 5 minutes, stirring constantly. Remove from heat and add Irish cream liquor.

6. Use a bamboo skewer to poke holes in the cooled cake. Spoon glaze over the cake. Allow cake to absorb the glaze. Enjoy!

Onion Cheese Nachos

Servings: 6

Cooking Time: 10 Minutes

Ingredients:

- 1 Pound Beef, Ground
- 3 Cups Cheddar Cheese, Shredded
- 1 Green Bell Pepper, Diced
- 1/2 Cup Green Onion
- 1/2 Cup Red Onion, Diced
- 1 Large Bag Tortilla Chip

Directions:

1. Supply your smoker with wood pellets and follow the start-up procedure. Preheat the grill, with the lid closed, to 350° F.

2. While you're waiting, empty a large bag of nacho chips evenly onto a cast iron pan. Start loading up with toppings - cooked ground beef, red onion, red pepper, cheese, green onions. These are just the toppings we had on hand, so feel free to add anything you like! Make sure you do a couple layers of chips so everyone gets a good serving of nachos. And don't be skimpy with the cheese - lay it on heavy!

3. Place your loaded nachos on the grill and let the hot smoke melt your toppings into one cheesy creation. Heat at 350°F for 10 minutes or until the cheese has fully melted. Remove and serve with sour-cream and salsa.

Pound Cake

Servings: 8

Cooking Time: 60 Minutes

Ingredients:

- 1 1/2 Cup butter
- 8 Ounce cream cheese
- 3 Cup sugar
- 6 eggs
- 3 Teaspoon Bourbon Vanilla
- 1 Tablespoon lemon zest
- fresh strawberries
- whipped cream

Directions:

1. In a large bowl, cream the butter, cream cheese, and sugar. Add eggs one at a time, whipping in between. Add vanilla and lemon zest, whip.

2. Pour batter into greased loaf pans, about halfway full to allow cake to rise.

3. Supply your smoker with wood pellets and follow the start-up procedure. Preheat the grill, with the lid closed, to 325° F.

4. Place loaf pans on grill and cook for 1 hour - 1 hour and 15 minutes. Check the cake at 45 minutes, if golden brown, cover loosely with foil and continue to cook until a toothpick inserted comes out clean. Grill: 325 °F

5. Cool loaf in pan for 10 minutes before removing to a wire rack.

6. Cut into 1 inch slices and serve with fresh sliced strawberries, top with smoked whip cream.

Sweet Cheese Muffins

Servings: 3

Cooking Time: 15 Minutes

Ingredients:

- 1 package butter cake mix
- 1 package Jiffy Corn Muffin Mix
- 1 cup self-rising or cake flour
- 12 tablespoons (1½ sticks) unsalted butter, softened, plus 8 tablespoons (1 stick) melted
- 3½ cups shredded Cheddar cheese
- 2 eggs, beaten, at room temperature
- 2¼ cups buttermilk
- Nonstick cooking spray or butter, for greasing
- ¼ cup packed brown sugar

Directions:

1. Supply your smoker with wood pellets and follow the start-up procedure. Preheat, with the lid closed, to 375°F.

2. In a large mixing bowl, combine the cake mix, corn muffin mix, and flour.

3. Slice the 1½ sticks of softened butter into pieces and cut into the dry ingredients. Add the cheese and mix thoroughly.

4. In a medium bowl, combine the eggs and buttermilk, then add to the dry ingredients, stirring until well blended.

5. Coat three 12-cup mini muffin pans with cooking spray and spoon ¼ cup of batter into each cup.

6. Transfer the pans to the grill, close the lid, and smoke, monitoring closely, for 12 to 15 minutes, or until the muffins are lightly browned.

7. While the muffins are cooking, make the topping: In a small bowl, stir together the remaining 1 stick of melted butter and the brown sugar until well combined.

8. Remove the muffins from the grill. Brush the tops with the sweet butter and serve warm.

Skillet Buttermilk Cornbread

Servings: 6

Cooking Time: 25 Minutes

Ingredients:

- 1 Cup Cornmeal
- 1 Cup all-purpose flour
- 1/3 Cup granulated sugar
- 1 Teaspoon salt
- 1 Teaspoon baking powder
- 1 1/2 Cup buttermilk
- 2 Whole eggs
- 8 Tablespoon butter, melted

Directions:

1. Grease a cast iron skillet or 9-inch square baking pan with bacon fat. Put a 10-inch well-seasoned cast iron skillet on the grill grate. If using a regular baking pan, do not preheat.

2. Supply your smoker with wood pellets and follow the start-up procedure. Preheat the grill, with the lid closed, to 400° F.

3. In a large mixing bowl, combine the cornmeal, flour, sugar, salt, and baking powder and whisk to mix thoroughly. Make a well in the center of the dry ingredients.

4. In a separate mixing bowl, whisk together the buttermilk and eggs until well-combined. Add the melted butter. Pour into the dry ingredients and mix until the batter is fairly smooth. Do not overmix.

5. Carefully pour the batter into the preheated skillet. Bake for 20 to 25 minutes, or until the top is firm and a tester inserted in the center of the cornbread comes out clean. Be careful when removing the skillet from the grill as it will be very hot. Let the cornbread cool slightly on a trivet or cooling rack before slicing into wedges or squares.

Cinnamon Pull-aparts

Servings: 6

Cooking Time: 20 Minutes

Ingredients:

- 16.3 Ounce Biscuits, Homestyle, Canned
- 1 Cup packed brown sugar
- 1/2 Cup butter
- 1/4 Cup water
- 1 Teaspoon ground cinnamon
- 1/2 Cup Nuts (optional)

Directions:

1. Cut each biscuit into 4 pieces and peel each piece in half; set aside.

2. Combine brown sugar, butter and water in a large saucepan and bring to a boil; reduce heat and simmer for 1 minute. Stir in cinnamon and nuts; add biscuit quarters and mix to coat. Pour into greased 13 by 9 inch casserole dish and spread evenly in the dish.

3. Supply your smoker with wood pellets and follow the start-up procedure. Preheat the grill, with the lid closed, to 350° F.

4. Place the casserole dish on the grill; close lid and cook for 20 to 25 minutes or until the biscuits are done. Grill: 350 ℉

5. Remove from the grill and transfer to a serving platter making sure to get all the gooey syrup onto the biscuits. Serve warm. Enjoy!

Traeger Baked Protein Bars

Servings: 6

Cooking Time: 25 Minutes

Ingredients:

➢ 2 Cup Frozen Sweet Cherries

➢ 1 Cup Apricots, Frozen

➢ 1 Scoop Vanilla Protein Powder

➢ 2 Tablespoon honey

➢ 1 Teaspoon vanilla extract

➢ 1 Cup rolled oats

Directions:

1. Supply your smoker with wood pellets and follow the start-up procedure. Preheat the grill, with the lid closed, to 350° F.

2. In the bowl of a food processor, add cherries, apricots (revived in hot water for 5 minutes and drained), vanilla protein powder, honey, and vanilla. Pulse about 10 to 15 times, to break the fruit into smaller pieces and to mix all ingredients.

3. In a separate bowl, fold together oats and fruit mixture. Transfer mixture to a loaf pan or silicone mold and place in grill.

4. Bake for approximately 20 to 25 minutes. Grill: 350 °F

5. Let cool completely and cut into 8 pieces. Enjoy!

Irish Soda Bread

<table>
<tr><td>Servings: 8-12</td><td>Cooking Time: 45 Minutes</td></tr>
</table>

Ingredients:

- As Needed Cornmeal
- 3 1/2 Cup all-purpose flour
- 1 1/2 Teaspoon sugar
- 1 1/4 Teaspoon baking soda
- 1 Teaspoon salt
- 1 Cup buttermilk
- To Taste butter

Directions:

1. When ready to cook, set the temperature to 400F (205 C) and preheat, lid closed, for 10 to 15 minutes.

2. Lightly dust the bottom of an 8-inch (20-cm) round cake pan with cornmeal and set aside.

3. Tear off a large sheet of wax paper and lay it on your work surface.

4. Combine the flour, sugar, soda, and salt in a large sifter and sift onto the wax paper. Carefully lift up the sides of the wax paper and tip the flour mixture back into the sifter. Re-sift into a large mixing bowl.

5. Lightly flour your work surface. Make a well in the middle of the flour mixture in the bowl and pour in 1 cup (240 mL) of buttermilk. Stir with a wooden spoon. Work quickly and gently as the carbon dioxide bubbles formed when the buttermilk hits the dry ingredients will deflate, the dough will look somewhat shaggy. If the dough seems dryish, add a little more buttermilk.

6. Turn out onto the floured surface, and with floured hands, knead gently for 10 to 20 seconds - just long enough to bring the dough bits together. (It will look more like biscuit dough than bread dough.)

7. Form into a flattish round and transfer to the prepared pan. Flour a sharp knife, and deeply cut a cross in the top of the loaf all the way to the edge of the bread. Quickly get it in to bake, if it sits too long, it will deflate.

8. Bake the bread for 45 to 50 minutes, or until it is browned and the bottom of the loaf sounds hollow when rapped with your knuckles.

9. Remove the bread from the baking pan and cool on a cooling rack. Just be-fore serving, cut the loaf in half and then slice each half into thin slices.

10. Serve with butter. Wrap leftovers tightly in plastic wrap or foil. This bread makes great toast. Enjoy!

Baked Pear Tarte Tatin

Servings: 6

Cooking Time: 45 Minutes

Ingredients:

- 2 1/2 Cup all-purpose flour
- 2 Tablespoon sugar
- butter chilled
- 8 Tablespoon cold water
- 1/4 Cup granulated sugar
- 1/4 Cup butter
- 8 Whole Bartlett Pear

Directions:

1. Supply your smoker with wood pellets and follow the start-up procedure. Preheat the grill, with the lid closed, to 350° F.

2. For the crust: Place flour and sugar in a food processor and pulse to mix. Add butter a little at a time while pulsing. Once it starts to looks like cornmeal, add the water until dough start to come together.

3. Form a round with the dough, wrap in plastic and let it cool in the refrigerator.

4. While dough cools, make the caramel sauce. In a sauce pan, add 1/4 cup granulated sugar and 1/4 cup butter. Cook butter and sugar until it becomes a dark caramel, a couple minutes.

5. Pour caramel in the bottom of 10 inch deep cake pan. While the caramel is still hot, arrange pear wedges in a fan formation covering the caramel.

6. Roll the chilled pie dough into a circle big enough to cover the pan. Prick the pie dough with a fork and cover the pan with the pie dough. Trim the crust leaving room for shrinkage.

7. Place on the grill and bake for 45 minutes or until pears are soft. The pears will be soft and most of the juice will evaporate and thicken.

8. Let sit for 3 minutes. While pan is still hot, place a plate over pie and flip over. Slowly lift the plate.

9. Serve warm, topped with vanilla ice cream or whipped cream. Enjoy!

Traeger Baked Focaccia

Servings: 4

Cooking Time: 40 Minutes

Ingredients:

- 2 1/2 Cup all-purpose flour
- 1 Cup warm water (110°F to 115°F)
- 1 Tablespoon instant yeast
- 1 Teaspoon sugar
- 1 Teaspoon salt
- 3 Tablespoon olive oil, plus more as needed
- 1 Tablespoon fresh herbs such as thyme, rosemary and sage
- 2 Tablespoon freshly grated Parmesan, optional
- flaky sea salt

Directions:

1. Place the flour, water, yeast, sugar, salt and oil in the bowl of a stand mixer and mix for 60 seconds. You may also use a food processor by adding the flour, sugar, salt and yeast to the bowl and process while streaming in the warm water followed by the olive oil. Process until combined and a ball forms.

2. Gently form the sticky dough into a ball, if needed, and place in a well-oiled 12 inch cast iron skillet. Drizzle the top of the dough with more olive oil. Cover with plastic wrap and a kitchen towel and let rise in a warm spot for 45 to 60 minutes.

3. After the dough has risen, press the dough to the edges of the pan and cover it again. Let rise for 15 minutes.

4. Supply your smoker with wood pellets and follow the start-up procedure. Preheat the grill, with the lid closed, to 375° F.

5. Uncover the dough and press it again to the edges of the pan using your fingertips to create divots.

6. Drizzle with olive oil, then sprinkle with herbs, Parmesan and flaky salt.

7. Bake it on the Traeger for 30 to 40 minutes, or until golden brown and cooked through. Allow it to cool slightly before removing from cast iron and slicing. Enjoy! Grill: 375 °F

Baked Parker House Rolls

Servings: 8	Cooking Time: 15 Minutes

Ingredients:

- 1/2 Ounce (2 packets) active dry yeast
- 6 Tablespoon plus 1 teaspoon cane sugar
- 1 Cup warm water (110°F to 115°F)
- 5 Cup all-purpose flour, plus more as needed
- 2 Teaspoon salt
- 1 Cup warm milk (110°-115°F)
- 1 Large eggs
- oil
- 4 Tablespoon melted butter, divided
- 1 Tablespoon Maldon Sea Salt Flakes
- 2 Tablespoon poppy seeds
- 2 Tablespoon white sesame seeds
- 1 Tablespoon garlic flakes

Directions:

1. Place the yeast, 1 teaspoon of cane sugar and warm water in a mixing bowl or the base of a stand mixer. Stir to combine. Allow the yeast to proof for 5 minutes- it should start to bubble a bit, showing that the yeast is alive.

2. Sprinkle the flour, salt and remaining 6 tablespoons of sugar over the yeast mixture. Using a dough hook or a wooden spoon, stir for 30 seconds. Pour in the warm milk and egg.

3. Knead again on the medium-low setting, or on a floured work surface by hand until the dough is very soft, adding up to one more cup of flour so the dough is soft and smooth and has lost its sticky quality.

4. Coat the bowl with a small film of oil and place the dough in the bowl, turning to coat dough evenly with the oil. Cover the bowl with a clean cloth, place in a warm spot in the kitchen and allow to proof about 45 minutes. The dough will almost double in size.

5. Punch down the dough and place on a floured work surface. Divide the dough in half, then divide each half into 12 equal pieces.

6. Using your hands, tuck in the seams of each piece of dough then place the dough on a lightly floured surface.

7. Place your fingers around the piece of dough, and roll it in a circular motion to create a smooth, even ball. Alternately, roll the dough between your two hands to create a round ball shape. Repeat with the remaining 23 pieces.

8. Butter a 9x13 inch baking pan with a tablespoon of the melted butter. Place the dough balls evenly in the pan, creating rows of 4 pieces of dough across and 6 down. Cover again with a clean towel and allow the dough to rise in a warm spot, about 30 minutes longer.

9. While the dough is proofing, supply your smoker with wood pellets and follow the start-up procedure. Preheat the grill, with the lid closed, to 325° F. Brush the remaining 3 tablespoons of butter on the bread and sprinkle with the flake salt, seeds and garlic flakes.

10. Place the pan on the grill, cover and bake about 15 to 20 minutes, or until rolls are lightly browned on top and cooked through. When done, you should be able to pull apart two pieces and see that the dough is cooked and the bottoms are lightly browned. Grill: 325 °F

Marbled Brownies With Amaretto & Ricotta

Servings: 4	Cooking Time: 30 Minutes

Ingredients:

- ➢ 1 Cup Ricotta Cheese
- ➢ 1 eggs
- ➢ 1 Tablespoon Amaretto Liqueur
- ➢ 1/4 Cup sugar
- ➢ 2 Teaspoon cornstarch
- ➢ 1/2 Teaspoon vanilla extract
- ➢ 1 Brownie Mix

Directions:

1. Coat a 9- by 13-inch nonstick baking pan with cooking spray or softened butter and set aside. (If you do not have a nonstick pan, line a regular one with buttered foil or parchment paper.)

2. In a medium bowl, combine the ricotta, egg, amaretto, sugar, cornstarch, and vanilla and whisk together thoroughly. Set aside.

3. Prepare the brownie mix according to the package directions. Spread the brownie batter evenly in the prepared pan. Randomly drop dollops of the ricotta mixture over the batter. Run a plastic knife through the ricotta mixture to give the brownies a marbled look. (A plastic knife is less likely to scratch your pan's nonstick surface.)

4. Supply your smoker with wood pellets and follow the start-up procedure. Preheat the grill, with the lid closed, to 350° F.

5. Put the pan with the brownie mixture directly on the grill grate and bake, about 25 to 30 minutes. Insert a bamboo skewer or toothpick in the center of the brownies to determine if they are done: the batter should not be wet. Grill: 350 °F

6. Transfer the brownies to a wire cooling rack to cool completely. Cut into squares.

PORK RECIPES

Savory Pork Belly Banh Mi

Servings: 4   Cooking Time: 420 Minutes

Ingredients:

- 2 Carrots, Sliced
- 1 Tbsp Cilantro, Minced
- 1 Tbsp Honey
- 2 Kirby Cucumbers, Sliced Thin
- 1 Lime, Zest & Juice
- 2 Tbsp Pickling Spice
- 1 Tbsp Ponzu
- 2 Lbs Pork Belly
- 1 Cup Rice Wine Vinegar
- 2 Tbsp Salt
- 4 Sandwich Buns
- 1 Small Daikon Radish, Sliced Thin
- To Taste, Smoky Salt & Cracked Pepper Rub
- 2 Tbsp Soy Sauce
- 1/2 Cup Sriracha Hot Sauce
- 4 Cloves Star Anise
- 1/2 Cup Sugar
- 1 Cup Water

Directions:

1. 30 minutes before you plan to put the belly on the smoker season liberally with the Smoky Salt and Cracked Pepper rub.

2. Supply your smoker with wood pellets and follow the start-up procedure. Preheat the grill, with the lid open, to 240° F. If using a gas or charcoal grill, set it up for low, indirect heat.

3. Place the belly on the smoker with a tin pan underneath the meat to catch the drippings. Smoke for 7 hours or until you reach an internal temp of 195 degrees. Remove the pork and let rest for 30 minutes.

4. Make the homemade pickles: Place pickling spice and star anise in a small sauce pan and toast. Once fragrant add vinegar and bring to a boil, cook for 3 minutes. Add the water, sugar, and salt and return to a boil, cook for 5 minutes. Strain the liquid and immediately pour over the vegetables, making sure the vegetables are submerged. Set in the fridge once cool.

5. Make the Sriracha Lime Sauce: Combine the sriracha, lime, soy sauce, honey, cilantro and ponzu in a mixing bowl and whisk until combined.

6. Assemble the sandwiches, placing sliced pork belly and homemade pickles on a roll before topping it with the sriracha lime sauce.

Maple-smoked Pork Chops

Servings: 4

Cooking Time: 55 Minutes

Ingredients:

➢ 1 (12-pound) full packer brisket

➢ 2 tablespoons yellow mustard

➢ 1 batch Espresso Brisket Rub

➢ Worcestershire Mop and Spritz, for spritzing

Directions:

1. Supply your smoker with wood pellets and follow the start-up procedure. Preheat the grill, with the lid closed, to 180°F.

2. Season the pork chops on both sides with salt and pepper.

3. Place the chops directly on the grill grate and smoke for 30 minutes.

4. Increase the grill's temperature to 350°F. Continue to cook the chops until their internal temperature reaches 145°F.

5. Remove the pork chops from the grill and let them rest for 5 minutes before serving.

Whiskey- & Cider-brined Pork Shoulder

Servings: 8   Cooking Time: 540 Minutes

Ingredients:

- 1 bone-in pork shoulder, about 5 to 7lb (2.3 to 3.2kg)
- fresh coarsely ground black pepper
- granulated garlic
- 1 cup apple juice or apple cider
- low-carb barbecue sauce, warmed
- hamburger buns (optional)
- for the brine
- 1 gallon (3.8 liters) cold distilled water
- 1 cup coarse salt
- 1¼ cup whiskey, divided
- ½ cup light brown sugar or low-carb substitute

Directions:

1. In a large saucepot on the stovetop over medium-high heat, make the brine by bringing the water, salt, 1 cup of whiskey, and brown sugar to a boil. Stir with a long-handled wooden spoon until the salt and sugar dissolve. Let the brine cool to room temperature. Cover and cool completely in the refrigerator.

2. Submerge the pork in the brine. If it floats, place a resealable bag of ice on top. Refrigerate for 24 hours.

3. Supply your smoker with wood pellets and follow the start-up procedure. Preheat the grill, with the lid closed, to 250° F.

4. Remove the pork shoulder from the brine and pat dry with paper towels. (Discard the brine.) Season the pork with pepper and granulated garlic. Place the pork on the grate and smoke until the internal temperature reaches 165°F (74°C), about 5 hours.

5. Transfer the pork to an aluminum foil roasting pan and add the apple juice and the remaining ¼ cup of whiskey. Cover tightly with aluminum foil. Place the pan on the grate and cook the pork until the bone releases easily from the meat and the internal temperature reaches 200°F (93°C), about 3 hours more. (Be careful when lifting a corner of the foil to check on the roast because steam will escape.)

6. Remove the pan from the grill and let the pork rest for 20 minutes. Reserve the juices.

7. Wearing heatproof gloves, pull the pork into chunks. Discard the bone or any large lumps of fat. Pull the meat into shreds and transfer to a clean aluminum foil roasting pan. Moisten with the barbecue sauce or serve the sauce on the side. Stir in some of the drippings—not too much because you don't want the pork to be swimming in its juices. Serve on buns (if using).

Beer Braised Pork Belly And Beef

Servings: 4

Cooking Time: 90 Minutes

Ingredients:

- 1, Dark Beer, Any Brand
- 3 Cups Broth, Beef
- 1 Tablespoon Chinese Cooking Wine (Such As Shaoxing) Or Dry Sherry Wine
- 1 Teaspoon Chinese Five Spice Powder
- 2, Smashed Garlic, Cloves
- 1 Inch Knob Ginger, Peeled And Thinly Sliced
- 1 Onion, Sliced
- 2 Pounds Pork Belly, Cut Into 1 Inch Chunks
- 2 Tablespoons Rice Wine Vinegar
- 2 Tablespoons, Dark Soy Sauce, Low Sodium
- 3 Tablespoons Sugar

Directions:

1. Place a heavy dutch oven on a stovetop over medium high heat. Add the pork belly and brown on all sides, about 5 minutes. Once the pork belly has browned, add in the onion, ginger, and garlic, and stir well.

2. Pour the beer, beef broth, soy sauce, dark soy sauce, sugar, Chinese cooking wine, rice wine vinegar, and Chinese five spice powder into the pan. Place a lid on the pan and bring it to a boil. Once it boils, remove it from the heat.

3. Supply your smoker with wood pellets and follow the start-up procedure. Preheat the grill, with the lid open, to 325° F. Place the pan of pork belly on the grill and braise for 1 ½ hours, or until the pork belly is falling apart tender and glazed.

4. Remove the pork belly from the grill and serve immediately.

Pork Tenderloin With Bourbon Peaches

Servings: 6   Cooking Time: 27 Minutes

Ingredients:

- 2 pork tenderloins, about 2lb (1kg) total, trimmed of silver skin and excess fat
- extra virgin olive oil
- for the rub
- 3 tbsp coarse salt
- 3 tbsp freshly ground black pepper
- 3 tbsp smoked or regular paprika
- 3 tbsp granulated light brown sugar or low-carb substitute
- 2 tbsp instant coffee
- 1 tbsp granulated garlic
- 2 tsp ground cumin
- 1 tsp chili powder
- for the peaches
- 4 freestone peaches, about 1lb (450g) total, peeled, pitted, and sliced
- 1 tbsp freshly squeezed lemon juice
- ¼ cup unsalted butter
- 4 tbsp granulated light brown sugar or low-carb substitute
- 2 tbsp bourbon
- ½ tsp ground cinnamon
- ½ tsp pure vanilla extract
- pinch of coarse salt

Directions:

1. Supply your smoker with wood pellets and follow the start-up procedure. Preheat the grill, with the lid closed, to 400° F.

2. In a small bowl, make the rub by combining the ingredients. Coat the tenderloins in olive oil and season with the rub.

3. Place the peaches and lemon juice in a medium bowl, turning the peaches gently to coat. Measure the other ingredients and then take them and the peaches grill side.

4. Place 1 tablespoon of olive oil in the hot skillet and add the tenderloins. Quickly sear the pork, about 2 to 3 minute per side, turning as needed with tongs. When they're nicely browned, transfer the tenderloins to the grate. Cook until the internal temperature in the thickest part of the meat reaches 145°F (63°C), about 8 minutes. For moist meat, don't cook the tenderloins beyond 155°F (68°C).

5. Transfer the pork to a cutting board and tent with aluminum foil.

6. Replace the cast iron skillet with a clean one and close the grill lid to let it heat. Once hot, make the bourbon peaches by melting the butter. Add the brown sugar, bourbon, cinnamon, vanilla, and salt. Cook the mixture until it bubbles, about 5 to 8 minutes. Add the peaches and cook for 5 to 8 minutes more, turning the peaches carefully with a spoon to coat. Carefully transfer the skillet to a trivet or another heatproof surface.

7. Slice the pork on a diagonal into ½-inch (1.25cm) slices. Shingle the slices on a platter. Spoon the peaches around the pork or serve separately.

Smoked Bacon Roses

Servings: 2

Cooking Time: 60 Minutes

Ingredients:

➢ 1 Pack Bacon, Thick Cut

➢ 1 Dozen Roses, Fake

Directions:

1. Supply your smoker with wood pellets and follow the start-up procedure. Preheat the grill, with the lid open, to 225° F.

2. Roll each piece of bacon tightly, starting on the thicker side of the strip. Take a toothpick and skewer the middle of the bottom of the bacon roll to keep the bacon from unraveling. With a second toothpick, skewer the bacon roll so that the two toothpicks form an "X" at the bottom of the roll of bacon. Do this to every piece of bacon.

3. Place the bacon rolls directly on the grates of your preheated Grill and smoke for an hour, checking on them every 20 minutes.

4. While the bacon is smoking, rip the petals of the fake roses off of the steams.

5. Once the bacon is fully cooked, remove the toothpicks and pierce the bacon in the head of the steam (where the fake flowers once were). If the bacon isn't staying, you can break a toothpick in half and stick it in the tip of the steam, press firmly and try piercing the bacon again.

6. Place in a nice vase with some babies breath and gift to your Valentine.

Raspberry Spiral Ham With Glaze

Servings: 12

Cooking Time: 120 Minutes

Ingredients:

➢ 1 Ham, Spiral (Precooked)

➢ Raspberry Chipotle Spice Rub

➢ 1/2 Jar Raspberry Jam

➢ 1 Quart Raspberry, Fresh

➢ 1/4 Cup Sugar

➢ 1/3 Cup Water, Warm

Directions:

1. Supply your smoker with wood pellets and follow the start-up procedure. Preheat the grill, with the lid open, to 225° F.

2. Season the ham with Raspberry Chipotle Spice, taking care to season in between each slice. Place in your Grill and smoke for about 2 hours.

3. Just before you pull the ham, combine glaze ingredients in a saucepan over medium heat until raspberries are no longer whole and the glaze is runny. If you want a smoother glaze, remove the raspberry seeds by draining the glaze through cheesecloth.

4. Pour glaze over the ham just before serving. Slice and serve hot. Enjoy!

Crown Roast Of Pork

Servings: 4

Cooking Time: 60 Minutes

Ingredients:

- 1 Whole Crown Roast of Pork, 12-14 ribs
- 1/4 Cup Pork & Poultry Rub
- 1 Cup apple juice
- 1 Cup Apricot BBQ Sauce

Directions:

1. Supply your smoker with wood pellets and follow the start-up procedure. Preheat the grill, with the lid closed, to 375° F.

2. Season the pork roast liberally with Traeger Pork and Poultry Rub. Let sit at room temperature for 30 minutes. Wrap each tip of the crown roast in a small piece of aluminum foil. This will protect the bones during the cook and prevent them from turning black.

3. Place the roast directly on the grill grate and cook for about 90 minutes spraying with apple juice every 30 minutes or so.

4. When the roast reaches an internal temperature of 125 degrees F, remove the aluminum foil from the bones and return to the grill.

5. Spray again with apple juice and continue to cook until the internal temperature reaches 135 degrees F in the thickest part of the roast. In the last ten minutes, baste the roast with the Apricot BBQ Sauce to let the glaze set.

6. Remove from the grill, tent with foil, and let it rest 15-20 minutes before slicing. Enjoy!

Bangers And Potato Mash

Servings: 6 - 8

Cooking Time: 135 Minutes

Ingredients:

- Bbq Sauce
- ¼ Cup Butter
- 3 Garlic, Cloves
- 1 Onion, Chopped
- 8 Red Potatoes, Medium
- 8 Sausages, Pork
- ½ Cup Milk

Directions:

1. Using a fork, poke holes all over every red potato.
2. Cut a whole bulb of garlic in half and set aside.
3. Supply your smoker with wood pellets and follow the start-up procedure. Preheat the grill, with the lid open, to 300° F.
4. Set the halved garlic bulb and red potatoes on the grill. Cook the garlic for 30 minutes and the potatoes for 75 minutes.
5. Turn your down to 250°F and allow it to settle to that temperature.
6. Peel and mash the potatoes and garlic with butter and milk until the desired smoothness is achieved.
7. Set the sausages on the grill and smoke for 1 hour.
8. Sauté sliced onions in a pan with butter and barbecue sauce to taste.
9. After 1 hour, remove the sausages and turn off the grill. Place the onions on top of the mash potatoes and the sausage on top of the onions. Add more BBQ sauce if you wish.

Beer-braised Cabbage With Bacon

Servings: 4

Cooking Time: 30 Minutes

Ingredients:

- 1/4 Pound Bacon, bulk unsliced
- 1 Cup yellow onion, diced
- 1 Cup Apple, diced small
- 2 Pound Cabbage, green, sliced
- salt
- ground black pepper
- 12 Ounce Beer, light

Directions:

1. Supply your smoker with wood pellets and follow the start-up procedure. Preheat the grill, with the lid closed, to 325° F.

2. On a stovetop, heat a large heavy pot or Dutch oven over medium heat. Add the bacon and cook until crisp (about 5 mins). Transfer to a plate lined with paper towels.

3. Return the pot to medium heat. Add the onion and cook for 5 minutes, or until golden brown. Add the apple, stir, then add the cabbage. Sprinkle generously with salt and a touch of black pepper and stir for 3 minutes.

4. Pour in the beer and bring to a boil over medium-high heat. Cover and move the pot immediately into the Traeger.

5. Cook at 325 degrees F (160 C) for 10 minutes. Remove lid and cook for an additional 10-15 more minutes, or until cabbage is tender and most of the liquid has evaporated. Grill: 325 °F

6. Add the reserved bacon and stir into the cabbage. Enjoy!

Beer Pork Belly Chili Con Carne

Servings: 4   Cooking Time: 120 Minutes

Ingredients:

- Avocado, Diced
- 2 Bay Leaves
- 1 Lbs Beef Stew Meat
- 12 Oz Beef Stock
- 12 Oz Beer, Bottle
- 15 Oz Black Beans, Rinsed And Drained
- 3 Tbsp Chili Powder
- Cilantro, Chopped
- 1 Tsp Coriander, Ground
- 2 Tsp Cumin, Ground
- 1 Tbsp Flour
- 4 Garlic Cloves, Minced
- 2 Tsp Mexican Oregano, Dried
- 2 Tbsp Olive Oil
- 2 Oz Pancetta, Diced
- Pork Belly, Cut Into 1 Inch Chunks
- 2 Red Onion, Chopped
- Rice, Cooked
- To Taste, Salt & Pepper
- Scallion, Sliced Thin
- 1/4 Cup Tomato Purée

Directions:

1. Supply your smoker with wood pellets and follow the start-up procedure. Preheat the grill, with the lid open, to 425° F. If using a gas or charcoal grill, set it up for medium-high heat. Place Dutch oven on grill and allow to preheat.

2. Heat the olive oil in the Dutch oven, then sauté the pancetta until crisp. Add the onions and sauté for 3 minutes, then add the garlic and sauté 1 minute, until fragrant. Remove mixture with a slotted spoon and set aside.

3. Add the pork belly and beef to the pot to brown, then add the chili powder, cumin, oregano, and coriander. Add the flour and cook for 2 minutes, stirring constantly.

4. Add the beer, beef stock, and tomato purée. Stir well, then return the pancetta mixture to the pot. Add the black beans and bay leaves, then season with salt and pepper.

5. Bring chili to a simmer, then reduce temperature to 325°F and simmer, uncovered, for 2 hours, stirring occasionally, until meat is tender, and sauce has thickened.

6. Remove the chili from the grill, then serve warm with cooked rice, avocado, fresh cilantro, and scallions.

Leftover Pulled Pork With Eggs

Servings: 4

Cooking Time: 20 Minutes

Ingredients:

- 1 Teaspoon Coarse Black Pepper
- 4 Eggs
- 1 Green Bell Pepper, Diced
- 1 Teaspoon Kosher Salt
- 3 Tablespoons Olive Oil
- 1 Small Onion, Diced
- 1 Tablespoon Hickory Bacon Seasoning
- 2 Cups Of Leftover Pulled Pork
- 1 Red Bell Peppers, Diced
- 1 ½ Pounds Red Potatoes, Diced

Directions:

1. Supply your smoker with wood pellets and follow the start-up procedure. Preheat the grill, with the lid open, to 350° F.

2. In a large bowl, toss the potatoes with 2 tablespoons of olive oil and Hickory Bacon seasoning. You want to get the potatoes coated well and evenly with the oil and seasoning.

3. Add the potatoes to the skillet and cook on the grill for 12-15 minutes or until they're cooked all the way through and browned. Remove from the pan and set aside.

4. Add 1 more tablespoon of olive to the pan and cook the peppers and onion for 2-3 minutes or until soft. Remove from the pan and set aside.

5. Add the pork to the pan and cook until warmed through. Because the pork is already cooked this should only be 1-2 minutes so the meat stays moist.

6. Add the potatoes, peppers and onions back to the pan, then give everything in the skillet a quick mix, so the hash is evenly blended.

7. Crack the 4 eggs on top of the hash. Try to space them evenly around. Sprinkle the teaspoons of salt and pepper on top of the eggs, then place the lid on top of the pan and allow the eggs to cook for 5-6 minutes, or until the whites are firm and the yolks are still runny.

8. Remove from the grill and serve immediately.

Spiced Grilled Pork Chops

Servings: 4

Cooking Time: 30 Minutes

Ingredients:

- 3 Tbsp Black Peppercorns, Ground
- 1 Tbsp Coriander, Seed
- 1/4 Cup Cumin
- 1 - 2 Tsp Dry Rub
- 1 Tsp Olive Oil
- 4 Pork, Chop Bone-In
- 1 1/2 Tsp Salt
- 2 Tbsp Sugar

Directions:

1. Supply your smoker with wood pellets and follow the start-up procedure. Preheat the grill, with the lid open, to 450° F.

2. Combine the cumin seeds, whole black peppercorns, and coriander seeds in a cast iron skillet. Stir over medium heat for about 8 minutes until toasted. Let them cool slightly. Finely grind toasted spices in a blender and transfer to a small bowl, then mix in sugar and salt.

3. Rub the spices into the pork chops on both sides. Place cast iron skillet inside the grill. Once hot, add the olive oil to the skillet and coat the bottom. Sprinkle the pork chops with salt, and then add to the skillet. Make sure that each pork chop has enough space in between one another. Cook the chops for about 30 minutes. Once pork chops are fully cooked, turn off the grill, remove skillet, plate and enjoy!

VEGETABLES RECIPES

Traeger Smoked Coleslaw

Servings: 8

Cooking Time: 20 Minutes

Ingredients:

- 1 Head purple cabbage, shredded
- 1 Head green cabbage, shredded
- 1 Cup shredded carrots
- 2 scallions, thinly sliced
- 1 1/2 Cup mayonnaise
- 1/8 Cup white wine vinegar
- 1 Teaspoon celery seed
- 1 Teaspoon sugar
- salt and pepper

Directions:

1. Supply your smoker with wood pellets and follow the start-up procedure. Preheat the grill, with the lid closed, to 180° F.

2. Spread cabbage and carrots out on a sheet tray and place directly on the grill grates. Smoke for 20 to 25 minutes or until cabbage picks up desired amount of smoke. Grill: 180 °F

3. Remove from grill and transfer to the refrigerator immediately to cool. While cabbage is cooling, make the dressing.

4. For the dressing, combine all ingredients in a small bowl and mix well.

5. Place smoked cabbage and carrots in a large bowl and pour dressing over them. Stir to coat well.

6. Transfer to a serving dish and sprinkle with scallions. Enjoy!

Grilled Beer Cabbage

Servings: 4

Cooking Time: 50 Minutes

Ingredients:

- ➤ 2 Cabbage, head
- ➤ 1 Tablespoon extra-virgin olive oil
- ➤ 1 Teaspoon salt
- ➤ 1 Teaspoon freshly ground black pepper
- ➤ 14 Fluid Ounce Guinness Extra Stout

Directions:

1. Clean and core cabbages. Drizzle with olive oil and salt and pepper. Rub into the cabbage.

2. Supply your smoker with wood pellets and follow the start-up procedure. Preheat the grill, with the lid closed, to 180° F.

3. Place cabbages directly on grill grate; smoke for 15 to 20 minutes. Remove from grill and thickly slice cabbage. Grill: 180 ˚F

4. Place sliced cabbage in cast-iron skillet. Pour beer over cabbage and return to grill.

5. Increase temperature to 375˚F and cook for 30 minutes, or until cabbage has reached desired softness. Grill: 375 ˚F

6. Serve with corned beef. Enjoy!

Roasted Potato Poutine

Servings: 6

Cooking Time: 40 Minutes

Ingredients:

- 4 Large russet potatoes
- Tablespoon olive oil or vegetable oil
- Prime Rib Rub
- Cup chicken or beef gravy (homemade or jarred)
- 1 1/2 Cup white or yellow cheddar cheese curds
- freshly ground black pepper
- 2 Tablespoon scallions

Directions:

1. Supply your smoker with wood pellets and follow the start-up procedure. Preheat the grill, with the lid closed, to 500° F.

2. Scrub the potatoes and slice into fries, wedges or preferred shape.

3. Put potatoes into a large mixing bowl and coat with oil. Season generously with Traeger Prime Rib rub.

4. Tip the potatoes onto a rimmed baking sheet and spread in a single layer, cut sides down.

5. Roast for 20 minutes, then using a spatula, turn the potatoes to the other cut side. Continue to roast until the potatoes are tender and golden brown, about 15 to 20 minutes more.

6. While potatoes cook, warm the gravy on the stovetop or in a heat-proof saucepan on your Traeger.

7. To assemble the poutine, arrange the potatoes in a large shallow bowl or on a serving platter. Distribute the cheese curds on top. Pour the hot gravy evenly over the potatoes and cheese curds.

8. Season with black pepper and garnish with thinly sliced scallions. Serve immediately. Enjoy!

Baked Artichoke Parmesan Mushrooms

Servings: 8

Cooking Time: 30 Minutes

Ingredients:

- 8 Cremini Mushroom Caps
- 6 1/2 Ounce artichoke hearts
- 1/3 Cup Parmesan cheese, grated
- 1/4 Cup mayonnaise
- 1/2 Teaspoon garlic salt
- your favorite hot sauce
- paprika

Directions:

1. Clean the mushrooms with a damp paper towel. Remove the stems and discard or save for another use.

2. Using a small spoon, scoop out the inside (gills, etc.). Combine the artichoke hearts, parmesan, mayonnaise, garlic salt, and hot sauce and mix well.

3. Mound the filling in the mushroom caps. Dust the tops with paprika.

4. Arrange the mushrooms in an oven-safe baking dish.

5. Supply your smoker with wood pellets and follow the start-up procedure. Preheat the grill, with the lid closed, to 350° F.

6. Bake the mushrooms (uncovered) until the filling is bubbling and just beginning to brown, about 25 to 30 minutes. Serve immediately. Grill: 350 ℉

7. For a simple variation, stuff the mushrooms with your favorite bulk sausage and bake on your Traeger as directed above. Enjoy!

Grilled Zucchini Squash Spears

Servings: 4

Cooking Time: 10 Minutes

Ingredients:

➢ 4 Medium zucchini

➢ 2 Tablespoon olive oil

➢ 1 Tablespoon sherry vinegar

➢ 2 thyme, leaves pulled

➢ salt and pepper

Directions:

1. Clean the zucchini and cut the ends off. Cut each in half lengthwise, then each half into thirds.

2. Combine remaining ingredients in a medium Ziplock bag and add the spears. Toss and mix well to coat the zucchini.

3. Supply your smoker with wood pellets and follow the start-up procedure. Preheat the grill, with the lid closed, to 350° F.

4. Remove the spears from the bag and place directly on the grill grate cut side down.

5. Cook for 3-4 minutes per side, until grill marks appear and zucchini is tender. Grill: 350 ℉

6. Remove from grill and finish with more thyme leaves if desired. Enjoy!

Salt Crusted Baked Potatoes

Servings: 4

Cooking Time: 60 Minutes

Ingredients:

- ➤ 6 russet potatoes, scrubbed and dried
- ➤ 3 Tablespoon canola oil
- ➤ 1 Tablespoon kosher salt
- ➤ butter
- ➤ sour cream
- ➤ Chives, fresh
- ➤ Bacon Bits
- ➤ cheddar cheese

Directions:

1. In a large bowl, coat the potatoes in canola oil and sprinkle heavily with salt.

2. Supply your smoker with wood pellets and follow the start-up procedure. Preheat the grill, with the lid closed, to 450° F.

3. Place the potatoes directly on the grill grate and bake for 30-40 minutes, or until soft in the middle when pricked with a fork. Serve loaded with your favorite toppings. Enjoy! Grill: 450 ˚F

Smoked Pico De Gallo

Servings: 4

Cooking Time: 30 Minutes

Ingredients:

- 3 Cup diced Roma tomatoes
- 1 jalapeño, diced
- 1/2 red onion, diced
- 1/2 Bunch cilantro, finely chopped
- 2 lime, juiced
- salt
- olive oil

Directions:

1. Supply your smoker with wood pellets and follow the start-up procedure. Preheat the grill, with the lid closed, to 180° F.

2. Place the diced tomatoes on a small sheet pan spreading them into a thin layer. Place the sheet pan directly on the grill and smoke for 30 minutes. Grill: 180 °F

3. When the tomatoes are finished, toss all ingredients in a medium bowl and finish with lime juice, salt and olive oil to taste. Serve and enjoy!

Roasted New Potatoes

Servings: 4

Cooking Time: 25 Minutes

Ingredients:

- 2 Pound small new potatoes
- 3 Tablespoon butter, melted
- 2 Tablespoon olive oil
- 2 Tablespoon whole mustard seeds
- salt and pepper
- 2 Tablespoon freshly minced chives
- 2 Tablespoon freshly minced parsley

Directions:

1. Place potatoes in a colander and rinse with cold water. Dry on paper towels and transfer to a rimmed baking sheet large enough to hold them in a single layer.
2. Drizzle the potatoes with butter and olive oil, then sprinkle them with the mustard seeds. Season with salt and pepper.
3. Supply your smoker with wood pellets and follow the start-up procedure. Preheat the grill, with the lid closed, to 400° F.
4. Place the baking sheet with the potatoes on the grill grate. Roast for about 25 minutes shaking the pan once or twice, until potatoes are tender and the skins are slightly wrinkled. Grill: 400 °F
5. Transfer potatoes to a bowl or platter. Top with fresh chives and parsley. Enjoy!

Roasted Artichokes With Garlic Butter

Servings: 2

Cooking Time: 60 Minutes

Ingredients:

➢ 2 Large artichokes

➢ 3 Tablespoon olive oil

➢ sea salt

➢ 1 Stick unsalted butter

➢ 2 Clove garlic, chopped

➢ 2 Tablespoon chives, parsley, tarragon or cilantro

➢ 1 lemon

Directions:

1. Supply your smoker with wood pellets and follow the start-up procedure. Preheat the grill, with the lid closed, to 375° F.

2. Meanwhile, break off and discard any small outer leaves on the artichokes. Use a knife to slice off the tops of the artichokes, then using scissors, cut off any thorns on the remaining artichoke leaves. Trim the very bottom of the stem, then peel the tough and fibrous outer layer of the stem. Finally, cut artichokes in half and rinse off.

3. Transfer artichokes to a large mixing bowl, drizzle with olive oil and generously sprinkle with sea salt. Toss to coat the artichokes thoroughly. Grill: 375 ˚F

4. Add the artichokes to the grill, cut side down, and roast at 375˚F until the artichoke bottoms are tender when poked with a fork or knife, about 50 to 60 minutes. Grill: 375 ˚F

5. When artichokes are almost done, add butter, chopped garlic and a pinch of sea salt to a small sauce pan and melt slowly over medium-low heat. Once the butter melts all the way and starts to bubble slightly, add the herbs.

6. When the artichokes are done, transfer to a butcher paper lined tray with the cut sides up. Drizzle half the garlic butter and squeeze half of the lemon over the artichokes. Add a small sprinkle of sea salt over the artichokes.

7. Serve with a ramekin of the remaining butter for dipping and extra wedges of lemon. Enjoy! Chef Tip: You can also serve with a ramekin of good mayonnaise mixed with a bit of hot sauce.

Smoked Pickled Green Beans

Servings: 4

Cooking Time: 45 Minutes

Ingredients:

- ➢ 1 Pound Green Beans, blanched
- ➢ 1/2 Cup salt
- ➢ 1/2 Cup sugar
- ➢ 1 Tablespoon red pepper flakes
- ➢ 2 Cup white wine vinegar
- ➢ 2 Cup ice water

Directions:

1. Supply your smoker with wood pellets and follow the start-up procedure. Preheat the grill, with the lid closed, to 180° F.

2. Place the blanched green beans on a mesh grill mat and place mat directly on the grill grate. Smoke the green beans for 30-45 minutes until they've picked up the desired amount of smoke. Remove from grill and set aside until the brine is ready. Grill: 180 ˚F

3. In a medium sized saucepan, bring all remaining ingredients, except ice water, to a boil over medium high heat on the stove. Simmer for 5-10 minutes then remove from heat and steep 20 minutes more. Pour brine over ice water to cool.

4. Once brine has cooled, pour over the green beans and weigh them down with a few plates to ensure they are completely submerged. Let sit 24 hours before use. Enjoy!

Stuffed Jalapenos

Servings: 8

Cooking Time: 60 Minutes

Ingredients:

- ➤ 40 Whole jalapeño
- ➤ 8 Ounce cream cheese, room temperature
- ➤ 1 Cup Sharp Cheddar Grated
- ➤ 1 1/2 Teaspoon Pork & Poultry Rub
- ➤ 2 Tablespoon sour cream
- ➤ 1 Whole (14 oz) cocktail sausages
- ➤ 20 Whole Slices of Smoked Bacon, Cut in Half

Directions:

1. Wash and dry the peppers. Cut the stem ends off with a paring knife, and using the same knife or a small metal spoon, carefully scrape the seeds and ribs out of each pepper. Set aside.

2. In a small bowl, combine the cream cheese, grated cheese, Traeger Pork and Poultry Rub, and the sour cream.

3. Transfer the mixture to a sturdy resealable plastic bag and trim 1/2-inch off one of the lower corners with a scissors. Squeeze the cream cheese mixture into each pepper, filling each a little over the halfway point.

4. Stuff one sausage into each pepper. Wrap the outside of each with a piece of bacon, securing with 1 or 2 toothpicks.

5. Arrange the peppers on a foil-lined baking sheet. Supply your smoker with wood pellets and follow the start-up procedure. Preheat the grill, with the lid closed, to 180° F, and smoke the peppers for 1 to 1-1/2 hours.

6. Increase the heat to 350 degrees F and continue to cook for 20 to 30 minutes, or until the bacon begins to render its fat and crisp. Enjoy! Grill: 350 °F

Roasted Olives

Servings: 4

Cooking Time: 45 Minutes

Ingredients:

- ➢ 2 Cup mixed olives
- ➢ 3 Sprig fresh rosemary
- ➢ 2 Clove garlic, minced
- ➢ 2 Tablespoon orange zest
- ➢ 1/3 Cup extra-virgin olive oil
- ➢ 2 Tablespoon orange juice
- ➢ 1/2 Teaspoon red pepper flakes

Directions:

1. Combine the olives, rosemary, garlic, orange zest, red pepper flakes, olive oil, and orange juice in a glass oven-safe pie plate or baking dish. Cover with foil.

2. Supply your smoker with wood pellets and follow the start-up procedure. Preheat the grill, with the lid closed, to 300° F.

3. Roast the olives for 45 minutes, stirring once or twice. Serve warm in an attractive bowl. Enjoy! Grill: 300 °F

Grilled Broccoli Rabe

Servings: 4

Cooking Time: 10 Minutes

Ingredients:

- ➤ 4 Tablespoon extra-virgin olive oil
- ➤ 4 Bunch broccoli rabe or broccolini
- ➤ kosher salt
- ➤ 1 lemon, halved

Directions:

1. Supply your smoker with wood pellets and follow the start-up procedure. Preheat the grill, with the lid closed, to 450° F.

2. On a platter or in a mixing bowl, drizzle the olive oil over the broccoli rabe. Use your hands to mix thoroughly, coating the vegetables evenly with the oil. Season with sea salt.

3. Place the broccoli rabe in one layer directly on the lowest grill grate. Close the lid and cook for 5 to 10 minutes. You want there to be some color and slight char on the first side. Flip and cook for a few more minutes. Grill: 450 ˚F

4. Transfer the broccoli rabe to a serving platter and squeeze the juice of half a lemon evenly over the top.

5. Serve with more lemon wedges on the side. Enjoy!

POULTRY RECIPES

Grilled Honey Chicken Wings

Servings: 4 - 8

Cooking Time: 30 Minutes

Ingredients:

- 2 Chipotles Chopped In Adobo
- 1 Apple Cider Vinegar
- 2 Tablespoons Balsamic Vinegar
- ¼ Cup Brown Sugar
- 2 ½ Lbs Chicken Wings, Trimmed And Patted Dry
- ¼ Cup Honey
- ½ Cup Ketchup
- ¼ Cup Adobo Sauce
- 2 Tablespoons Sweet Rib Rub
- 2 Teaspoons Worcestershire Sauce

Directions:

1. Supply your smoker with wood pellets and follow the start-up procedure. Preheat the grill, with the lid open, to 350° F. If you're using a charcoal or gas grill, set up the grill for medium high heat.

2. In a large bowl, whisk together the apple cider vinegar, ketchup, brown sugar, honey, chopped chipotle peppers with adobo sauce, balsamic vinegar, Worcestershire sauce, and Sweet Rib Rub. Whisk the glaze until it's well combined.

3. Add the wings to the glaze and place the bowl in the refrigerator. Marinade the chicken wings for up to 12 hours. Once the wings have finished marinating, remove the chicken wings from the marinade and place the chicken wings onto the wing rack.

4. Once all the wings have been placed on the wing rack, place the wing rack on the grill. Insert a temperature probe into the thickest part into one of the wings and grill the wings for 5 minutes, and then rotate the rack 180° and grill for another 5 minutes. Remove the wings once they have an internal temperature of 165°F and the juice from the chicken runs clear.

5. Remove the wings from the grill and serve immediately.

Sweet And Spicy Smoked Wings

Servings: 2-4

Cooking Time: 85 Minutes

Ingredients:

- ➤ 1 pound chicken wings
- ➤ 1 batch Sweet and Spicy Cinnamon Rub
- ➤ 1 cup barbecue sauce

Directions:

1. Supply your smoker with wood pellets and follow the start-up procedure. Preheat the grill, with the lid closed, to 325°F.

2. Season the chicken wings with the rub. Using your hands, work the rub into the meat.

3. Place the wings directly on the grill grate and cook until they reach an internal temperature of 165°F.

4. Transfer the wings into an aluminum pan. Add the barbecue sauce and stir to coat the wings.

5. Reduce the grill's temperature to 250°F and put the pan on the grill. Smoke the wings for 1 hour more, uncovered. Remove the wings from the grill and serve immediately.

Traditional Smoked Thanksgiving Turkey

Servings: 8

Cooking Time: 240 Minutes

Ingredients:

- 1/2 Pound butter
- 6 Clove garlic, minced
- 8 Sprig fresh thyme
- 1 Sprig fresh rosemary
- 1 Tablespoon cracked black pepper
- 1/2 Tablespoon kosher salt
- 20 Pound Turkey, Whole Birds (18-20 lbs)

Directions:

1. Supply your smoker with wood pellets and follow the start-up procedure. Preheat the grill, with the lid closed, to 300° F.

2. In a small bowl, combine softened butter with minced garlic, thyme leaves, chopped rosemary, black pepper and kosher salt.

3. Prep the turkey by separating the skin from the breast creating a pocket to stuff the butter-herb mixture in. Cover the entire breast with 1/4" thickness of butter mixture.

4. Season the whole turkey with kosher salt and black pepper. Optional: Stuff turkey cavity with Traditional Stuffing recipe. When ready to cook, set the grill temperature to 300℉ and preheat, lid closed for 15 minutes.

5. Place turkey on the grill and smoke for 3-4 hours. Check the internal temperature, the desired temperature is 175℉ in the thigh next to the bone, and 160℉ in the breast. Turkey will continue to cook once taken off grill to reach a final temperature of 165℉ in the breast. Grill: 300 ℉ Probe: 160 ℉

6. Let rest for 10-15 minutes before serving. Enjoy!

Applewood-smoked Whole Turkey

Servings: 6-8

Cooking Time: 300 Minutes

Ingredients:

- 1 (10- to 12-pound) turkey, giblets removed
- Extra-virgin olive oil, for rubbing
- ¼ cup poultry seasoning
- 8 tablespoons (1 stick) unsalted butter, melted
- ½ cup apple juice
- 2 teaspoons dried sage
- 2 teaspoons dried thyme

Directions:

1. Supply your smoker with wood pellets and follow the start-up procedure. Preheat, with the lid closed, to 250°F.

2. Rub the turkey with oil and season with the poultry seasoning inside and out, getting under the skin.

3. In a bowl, combine the melted butter, apple juice, sage, and thyme to use for basting.

4. Put the turkey in a roasting pan, place on the grill, close the lid, and grill for 5 to 6 hours, basting every hour, until the skin is brown and crispy, or until a meat thermometer inserted in the thickest part of the thigh reads 165°F.

5. Let the bird rest for 15 to 20 minutes before carving.

Bbq Chicken Breasts

Servings: 6

Cooking Time: 25 Minutes

Ingredients:

- ➢ 6 boneless, skinless chicken breast
- ➢ 1 1/2 Cup Sweet & Heat BBQ Sauce
- ➢ salt and pepper
- ➢ 1 Tablespoon chopped parsley, for garnish

Directions:

1. Place chicken breasts and 1 cup of Traeger Sweet & Heat BBQ Sauce in a resealable bag or large bowl, and gently turn to cover chicken evenly in the sauce. Marinate in the refrigerator overnight.

2. Supply your smoker with wood pellets and follow the start-up procedure. Preheat the grill, with the lid closed, to 450° F.

3. Remove chicken from marinade and season with salt and pepper.

4. Place chicken directly on the grill grate and cook for 10 minutes on each side flipping once or until internal temperature reaches 150°F.

5. Brush on remaining 1/2 cup of Traeger Sweet & Heat BBQ Sauce while chicken is still on the grill, and continue to cook 5 to 10 minutes longer or until a finished internal temperature of 165°F.

6. Remove chicken from grill and let rest 5 minutes before serving. Sprinkle with chopped parsley. Enjoy!

Spicy Bbq Whole Chicken

Servings: 4

Cooking Time: 180 Minutes

Ingredients:

- ➢ 6 Thai chiles
- ➢ 2 Tablespoon sweet paprika
- ➢ 1 Scotch bonnet pepper
- ➢ 2 Tablespoon sugar
- ➢ 3 Tablespoon salt
- ➢ 1 white onion
- ➢ 5 Clove garlic
- ➢ 4 Cup grapeseed oil
- ➢ 1 whole chicken

Directions:

1. In a food processor or blender, puree the Thai chiles, paprika, Scotch bonnet pepper, sugar, salt, onion, garlic and grapeseed oil together until smooth.

2. Smother the chicken with mixture and let rest in fridge overnight.

3. Supply your smoker with wood pellets and follow the start-up procedure. Preheat the grill, with the lid closed, to 300° F.

4. Place chicken on grill, breast side up and smoke for 3 hours, or until it reaches an internal temperature of 165°F in the breast. Grill: 300 °F Probe: 165 °F

5. Remove from grill and allow to rest for 10 to 15 minutes before slicing. Serve with sides of choice. Enjoy!

Sweet Cajun Wings

Servings: 4

Cooking Time: 30 Minutes

Ingredients:

- ➤ 2 Pound chicken wings
- ➤ Pork & Poultry Rub
- ➤ Cajun Shake

Directions:

1. Coat wings in Traeger Sweet rub and Traeger Cajun shake.

2. Supply your smoker with wood pellets and follow the start-up procedure. Preheat the grill, with the lid closed, to 350° F.

3. Cook for 30 minutes or until skin is brown and center is juicy and an instant-read thermometer reads at least 165°F. Serve, enjoy! Grill: 350 °F Probe: 165 °F

Bbq Chicken Thighs

Servings: 4

Cooking Time: 35 Minutes

Ingredients:

- ➢ 6 bone-in, skin-on chicken thighs
- ➢ salt and ground black pepper
- ➢ Big Game Rub

Directions:

1. Supply your smoker with wood pellets and follow the start-up procedure. Preheat the grill, with the lid closed, to 350° F.

2. While grill is heating, trim excess fat and skin from chicken thighs. Season with a light layer of salt and pepper then a layer of Traeger Big Game Rub.

3. Place chicken thighs on the grill grate and cook for 35 minutes. Check internal temperature, chicken is done at 165°F, but there is enough fat that they will stay moist at an internal temperature of 180°F and the texture is better. Grill: 350 °F Probe: 165 °F

4. Remove from the grill and let rest for 5 minutes before serving. Enjoy!

Lemon & Herb Chicken

Servings: 3-4

Cooking Time: 75 Minutes

Ingredients:

- 1 roaster chicken, about 4lb (1.8kg), preferably organic
- 1 large sweet onion, peeled and sliced lengthwise into 8 wedges
- ½ cup chicken stock or broth
- sprigs of fresh rosemary, thyme, parsley, tarragon, or chives (or a mix)
- lemon wedges
- for the butter
- 4 tbsp unsalted butter, at room temperature
- 1 garlic clove, peeled and finely minced
- 2 tbsp chopped fresh herbs, such as rosemary, thyme, parsley, tarragon, or chives (or a mix)
- 2 tsp lemon zest
- 2 tsp freshly squeezed lemon juice
- ½ tsp coarse salt
- ½ tsp freshly ground black pepper

Directions:

1. Supply your smoker with wood pellets and follow the start-up procedure. Preheat the grill, with the lid closed, to 400° F.

2. In a small bowl, make the herb butter by combining the ingredients.

3. Place the chicken on a rimmed sheet pan and tuck the lemon rinds from the butter into the main cavity. Rub the outside of the chicken with the herb butter. (Reserve any remainder.) Tuck the wings behind the back and tie the legs together with butcher's twine. Place the onion wedges in a shallow roasting pan to help form a natural rack for the chicken. (Alternatively, place several large carrots, trimmed and peeled, on the bottom of the pan.) Place the chicken on the onion rack. Add the chicken stock and any remaining herbed butter and lemon juice.

4. Place the roasting pan on the grate, roast the chicken for 30 minutes, and then baste with the juices from the bottom of the pan. Baste every 15 minutes until the chicken is golden brown and the internal temperature reaches 165°F (74°C), about 45 minutes more.

5. Transfer the chicken to a cutting board and let rest for 10 minutes. Carve the chicken and place the slices on a platter with a deep well. Spoon some of the juices over the chicken. Scatter fresh herbs over the top. Serve with the lemon wedges.

Roasted Christmas Goose

Servings: 8

Cooking Time: 120 Minutes

Ingredients:

- 5 1/2 Pound Goose
- 2 lemons
- 2 limes
- 2 Teaspoon salt
- 2 thyme sprigs
- 2 sage sprigs
- 1 Medium Apple, green
- 3 Tablespoon honey

Directions:

1. Supply your smoker with wood pellets and follow the start-up procedure. Preheat the grill, with the lid closed, to High heat.

2. Lightly score the breast and leg skin in a criss-cross pattern. This will help the fat to render down more quickly during cooking.

3. Grate the lemon and limes. Mix citrus zest with 2 teaspoons fine sea salt. Cut the lemons and lime into wedges.

4. Season cavity of the goose generously with salt, then rub the citrus mix well into the skin and sprinkle some inside the cavity.

5. Stuff goose with sage, thyme, lemons, limes and apples wedges. Place goose directly on the grill grate and cook for 40 minutes. Brush goose with honey and reduce temperature to 325°F.

6. Cook for 1-1/2 to 2 hours or until an instant read thermometer inserted in the thickest part of the breast reads 160°F. Grill: 325 °F Probe: 160 °F

7. Remove from grill, tent with foil and allow to rest for 30 minutes. Final internal temperature should be 165°F in the thickest part of the breast. Enjoy!

Smoked Honey Chicken Drumsticks

Servings: 4

Cooking Time: 30 Minutes

Ingredients:

- 1/2 Cup Apple Cider Vinegar
- 12 Chicken Drumsticks
- 2 Tablespoons Dijon Mustard
- 1/4 Cup Honey
- 1/4 Cup Ketchup
- 1 Tablespoon   Sweet Heat Rub
- 1/2 Cup Soy Sauce

Directions:

1. Supply your smoker with wood pellets and follow the start-up procedure. Preheat the grill, with the lid open, to 225° F. Remove the wings from the marinade and place the drumsticks into the   Buffalo Wing Rack.

2. Smoke for 60 minutes, or until a thermometer inserted into the thickest part of the drumstick registers at 170°F.

3. Turn the heat up to 350°F and cook for 5 to 10 minutes to make the skin crisp.

4. Remove from the smoker, serve immediately and enjoy!

Smoked Chicken Leg & Thigh Quarters

Servings: 6

Cooking Time: 120 Minutes

Ingredients:

- 8 chicken legs (thigh and drumstick)
- 3 Tablespoon olive oil
- Pork & Poultry Rub

Directions:

1. Place the chicken pieces in a large mixing bowl. Pour oil over the chicken to coat each piece, then season to taste with the Traeger Pork & Poultry Rub. Massage the chicken pieces to encourage the oil and seasonings get under the skin. Cover and refrigerate for at least 1 to 2 hours.

2. Supply your smoker with wood pellets and follow the start-up procedure. Preheat the grill, with the lid closed, to 180° F.

3. Remove the chicken from the refrigerator, letting any excess oil drip back into the bowl. Grill: 180 °F

4. Arrange the chicken on the grill grate and smoke for 1 hour. Increase Traeger temperature to 350°F and continue to roast the chicken until the internal temperature in the thickest part of a thigh is 165°F or the chicken is golden brown and the juices run clear, about 50 to 60 minutes. Grill: 350 °F Probe: 165 °F

5. Remove from the grill and allow the chicken to rest for 8 to 10 minutes and serve. Enjoy!

Smo-fried Chicken

Servings: 4-6

Cooking Time: 55 Minutes

Ingredients:

- 1 egg, beaten
- ½ cup milk
- 1 cup all-purpose flour
- 2 tablespoons salt
- 1 tablespoon freshly ground black pepper
- 2 teaspoons freshly ground white pepper
- 2 teaspoons cayenne pepper
- 2 teaspoons garlic powder
- 2 teaspoons onion powder
- 1 teaspoon smoked paprika
- 8 tablespoons (1 stick) unsalted butter, melted
- 1 whole chicken, cut up into pieces

Directions:

1. Supply your smoker with wood pellets and follow the start-up procedure. Preheat, with the lid closed, to 375°F.

2. In a medium bowl, combine the beaten egg with the milk and set aside.

3. In a separate medium bowl, stir together the flour, salt, black pepper, white pepper, cayenne, garlic powder, onion powder, and smoked paprika.

4. Line the bottom and sides of a high-sided metal baking pan with aluminum foil to ease cleanup.

5. Pour the melted butter into the prepared pan.

6. Dip the chicken pieces one at a time in the egg mixture, and then coat well with the seasoned flour. Transfer to the baking pan.

7. Smoke the chicken in the pan of butter ("smo-fry") on the grill, with the lid closed, for 25 minutes, then reduce the heat to 325°F and turn the chicken pieces over.

8. Continue smoking with the lid closed for about 30 minutes, or until a meat thermometer inserted in the thickest part of each chicken piece reads 165°F.

9. Serve immediately.

APPETIZERS AND SNACKS

Pig Pops (sweet-hot Bacon On A Stick)

Servings: 24

Cooking Time: 30 Minutes

Ingredients:

- ➢ Nonstick cooking spray, oil, or butter, for greasing
- ➢ 2 pounds thick-cut bacon (24 slices)
- ➢ 24 metal skewers
- ➢ 1 cup packed light brown sugar
- ➢ 2 to 3 teaspoons cayenne pepper
- ➢ ½ cup maple syrup, divided

Directions:

1. Supply your smoker with wood pellets and follow the start-up procedure. Preheat, with the lid closed, to 350°F.
2. Coat a disposable aluminum foil baking sheet with cooking spray, oil, or butter.
3. Thread each bacon slice onto a metal skewer and place on the prepared baking sheet.
4. In a medium bowl, stir together the brown sugar and cayenne.
5. Baste the top sides of the bacon with ¼ cup of maple syrup.
6. Sprinkle half of the brown sugar mixture over the bacon.
7. Place the baking sheet on the grill, close the lid, and smoke for 15 to 30 minutes.
8. Using tongs, flip the bacon skewers. Baste with the remaining ¼ cup of maple syrup and top with the remaining brown sugar mixture.
9. Continue smoking with the lid closed for 10 to 15 minutes, or until crispy. You can eyeball the bacon and smoke to your desired doneness, but the actual ideal internal temperature for bacon is 155°F
10. Using tongs, carefully remove the bacon skewers from the grill. Let cool completely before handling.

Citrus-infused Marinated Olives

Servings: 6

Cooking Time: 30 Minutes

Ingredients:

- 1½ cups mixed brined olives, with pits
- ½ cup extra virgin olive oil
- 1 tbsp freshly squeezed lemon juice
- 1 garlic clove, peeled and thinly sliced
- 1 tsp smoked Spanish paprika
- 2 sprigs of fresh rosemary
- 2 sprigs of fresh thyme
- 2 bay leaves, fresh or dried
- 1 small dried red chili pepper, deseeded and flesh crumbled, or ¼ tsp crushed red pepper flakes
- 3 strips of orange zest
- 3 strips of lemon zest

Directions:

1. Supply your smoker with wood pellets and follow the start-up procedure. Preheat the grill, with the lid closed, to 180° F.

2. Drain the olives, reserving 1 tablespoon of brine. Spread the olives in a single layer in an aluminum foil roasting pan. Place the pan on the grate and cook the olives for 30 minutes, stirring the olives or shaking the pan once or twice.

3. In a small saucepan on the stovetop over low heat, warm the olive oil. Whisk in the lemon juice and the reserved 1 tablespoon of brine. Stir in the garlic and paprika. Add the rosemary, thyme, bay leaves, chili pepper, and orange and lemon zests. Warm over low heat for 10 minutes. Remove the saucepan from the heat.

4. Transfer the olives and olive oil mixture to a pint jar. Tuck the aromatics around the sides of the jar. Let cool and then cover and refrigerate for up to 5 days. Let the olives come to room temperature before serving.

Chorizo Queso Fundido

Servings: 4-6   Cooking Time: 20 Minutes

Ingredients:

- 1 poblano chile
- 1 cup chopped queso quesadilla or queso Oaxaca
- 1 cup shredded Monterey Jack cheese
- ¼ cup milk
- 1 tablespoon all-purpose flour
- 2 (4-ounce) links Mexican chorizo sausage, casings removed
- ⅓ cup beer
- 1 tablespoon unsalted butter
- 1 small red onion, chopped
- ½ cup whole kernel corn
- 2 serrano chiles or jalapeño peppers, stemmed, seeded, and coarsely chopped
- 1 tablespoon minced garlic
- 1 tablespoon freshly squeezed lime juice
- 1 teaspoon ground cumin
- 1 teaspoon salt
- 1 teaspoon freshly ground black pepper
- 1 tablespoon chopped fresh cilantro
- 1 tablespoon chopped scallions
- Tortilla chips, for serving

Directions:

1. Supply your smoker with wood pellets and follow the start-up procedure. Preheat, with the lid closed, to 350°F.

2. On the smoker or over medium-high heat on the stove top, place the poblano directly on the grate (or burner) to char for 1 to 2 minutes, turning as needed. Remove from heat and place in a closed-up lunch-size paper bag for 2 minutes to sweat and further loosen the skin.

3. Remove the skin and coarsely chop the poblano, removing the seeds; set aside.

4. In a bowl, combine the queso quesadilla, Monterey Jack, milk, and flour; set aside.

5. On the stove top, in a cast iron skillet over medium heat, cook and crumble the chorizo for about 2 minutes.

6. Transfer the cooked chorizo to a small, grill-safe pan and place over indirect heat on the smoker.

7. Place the cast iron skillet on the preheated grill grate. Pour in the beer and simmer for a few minutes, loosening and stirring in any remaining sausage bits from the pan.

8. Add the butter to the pan, then add the cheese mixture a little at a time, stirring constantly.

9. When the cheese is smooth, stir in the onion, corn, serrano chiles, garlic, lime juice, cuvmin, salt, and pepper. Stir in the reserved chopped charred poblano.

10. Close the lid and smoke for 15 to 20 minutes to infuse the queso with smoke flavor and further cook the vegetables.

11. When the cheese is bubbly, top with the chorizo mixture and garnish with the cilantro and scallions.

12. Serve the chorizo queso fundido hot with tortilla chips.

Jalapeño Poppers With Chipotle Sour Cream

Servings: 8

Cooking Time: 45 Minutes

Ingredients:

- 3 strips of thin-sliced bacon
- 12 large jalapeños, red, green, or a mix
- 8oz (225g) light cream cheese, at room temperature
- 1 cup shredded pepper Jack, Monterey Jack, or Cheddar cheese
- 1 tsp chili powder
- ½ tsp garlic salt
- smoked paprika

- for the sour cream
- 1¼ cups light sour cream
- juice of ½ lime
- ½ to 1 canned chipotle peppers in adobo sauce, finely minced, plus 1 tsp of sauce, plus more
- 1 tbsp minced fresh cilantro leaves
- ½ tsp coarse salt, plus more

Directions:

1. Supply your smoker with wood pellets and follow the start-up procedure. Preheat the grill, with the lid closed, to 375° F.

2. Line a rimmed sheet pan with aluminum foil and place a wire rack on top. Place the bacon in a single layer on the wire rack. Place the pan on the grate and grill until the bacon is crisp and golden brown, about 20 minutes. Transfer the bacon to paper towels to cool and then crumble. Set aside.

3. In a small bowl, make the chipotle sour cream by whisking together the ingredients. Add more salt, chipotle peppers, or adobe sauce to taste. Cover and refrigerate.

4. Slice the jalapeños lengthwise through their stems. Scrape out the veins and seeds with the edge of a small metal spoon.

5. In a small bowl, beat together the cream cheese, shredded cheese, chili powder, and garlic salt. Stir in the crumbled bacon. Mound the cream cheese mixture in the jalapeño halves. Line another rimmed sheet pan with aluminum foil and place a wire rack on top. Place the jalapeños filled side up in a single layer on the wire rack.

6. Place the sheet pan on the grate and roast the jalapeños until the filling has melted and the peppers have softened, about 20 to 25 minutes. (They should no longer look bright in color.) Remove the pan from the grill and let the peppers rest for 5 minutes.

7. Transfer the poppers to a platter and lightly dust with paprika. Serve with the chipotle sour cream.

Bacon Pork Pinwheels (kansas Lollipops)

Servings: 4-6

Cooking Time: 20 Minutes

Ingredients:

- 1 Whole Pork Loin, boneless
- To Taste salt and pepper
- To Taste Greek Seasoning
- 4 Slices bacon
- To Taste The Ultimate BBQ Sauce

Directions:

1. When ready to cook, start the smoker and set temperature to 500F. Preheat, lid closed, for 10 to 15 minutes.

2. Trim pork loin of any unwanted silver skin or fat. Using a sharp knife, cut pork loin length wise, into 4 long strips.

3. Lay pork flat, then season with salt, pepper and Cavender's Greek Seasoning.

4. Flip the pork strips over and layer bacon on unseasoned side. Begin tightly rolling the pork strips, with bacon being rolled up on the inside.

5. Secure a skewer all the way through each pork roll to secure it in place. Set the pork rolls down on grill and cook for 15 minutes.

6. Brush BBQ Sauce over the pork. Turn each skewer over, then coat the other side. Let pork cook for another 5-10 minutes, depending on thickness of your pork. Enjoy!

Chuckwagon Beef Jerky

Servings: 6	Cooking Time: 300 Minutes

Ingredients:

- 2½lb (1.2kg) boneless top or bottom round steak, sirloin tip, flank steak, or venison
- 1 cup sugar-free dark-colored soda
- 1 cup cold brewed coffee
- ½ cup light soy sauce
- ¼ cup Worcestershire sauce
- 2 tbsp whiskey (optional)
- 2 tsp chili powder
- 1½ tsp garlic salt
- 1 tsp onion powder
- 1 tsp pink curing salt

Directions:

1. Slice the meat into ¼-inch-thick (.5cm) strips, trimming off any visible fat or gristle. (Slice against the grain for more tender jerky and with the grain for chewier jerky.) Place the meat in a large resealable plastic bag.

2. In a small bowl, whisk together the soda, coffee, soy sauce, Worcestershire sauce, whiskey (if using), chili powder, garlic salt, onion powder, and curing salt (if using). Whisk until the salt dissolves. Pour the mixture over the meat and reseal the bag. Refrigerate for 24 to 48 hours, turning the bag several times to redistribute the brine.

3. Supply your smoker with wood pellets and follow the start-up procedure. Preheat the grill, with the lid closed, to 150° F.

4. Drain the meat and discard the brine. Place the strips of meat in a single layer on paper towels and blot any excess moisture.

5. Place the meat in a single layer on the grate and smoke for 4 to 5 hours, turning once or twice. (If you're aware of hot spots on your grate, rotate the strips so they smoke evenly.) To test for doneness, bend one or two pieces in the middle. They should be dry but still somewhat pliant. Or simply eat a piece to see if it's done to your liking.

6. For the best texture, when you remove the meat from the grill, place the still-warm jerky in a resealable plastic bag and let rest for 30 minutes. (You might see condensation form on the inside of the bag, but the moisture will be reabsorbed by the meat.) Or let the meat cool completely and then store in a resealable plastic bag or covered container. The jerky will last a few days at room temperature but will last longer (up to 2 weeks) if refrigerated.

Bayou Wings With Cajun Rémoulade

Servings: 8   Cooking Time: 40 Minutes

Ingredients:

- 16 large whole chicken wings or 32 drumettes and flats, about 3lb (1.4kg) total
- for the rub
- 1 tbsp kosher salt
- 1 tsp freshly ground black pepper
- 1 tsp paprika
- ½ tsp ground cayenne, plus more
- ½ tsp garlic powder
- ½ tsp celery salt
- ½ tsp dried thyme
- 2 tbsp vegetable oil
- for the rémoulade
- 1¼ cups reduced-fat mayo
- ¼ cup Creole-style or whole grain mustard
- 2 tbsp horseradish
- 2 tbsp pickle relish
- 1 tbsp freshly squeezed lemon juice
- 1 tsp paprika, plus more
- 1 tsp hot sauce, plus more
- 1 tsp Worcestershire sauce
- coarse salt
- for serving
- lemon wedges
- pickled okra (optional)

Directions:

1. Supply your smoker with wood pellets and follow the start-up procedure. Preheat the grill, with the lid closed, to 350° F.

2. If using whole wings, cut through the two joints, separating them into drumettes, flats, and wing tips. (Discard the wing tips or save them for chicken stock.) Alternatively, leave the wings whole. Place the chicken in a resealable plastic bag.

3. In a small bowl, make the rub by combining the ingredients. Mix well. Pour the rub over the wings and toss them to thoroughly coat. Refrigerate for 2 hours.

4. In a small bowl, make the Cajun rémoulade by whisking together the mayo, mustard, horseradish, pickle relish, lemon juice, paprika, hot sauce, and Worcestershire. Season with salt to taste. The mixture should be highly seasoned. Transfer to a serving bowl and lightly dust with paprika. Cover and refrigerate until ready to serve.

5. Remove the wings from the refrigerator and allow the excess marinade to drip off. Place the wings on the grate at an angle to the bars. Grill for 20 minutes and then turn. (They'll brown more evenly but will also have less of a tendency to stick.) Continue to cook until the wings are nicely browned and the meat is no longer pink at the bone, about 20 minutes more.

6. Remove the wings from the grill and pile them on a platter. Serve with the Cajun rémoulade, lemon wedges, and pickled okra (if using).

Pigs In A Blanket

Servings: 4-6

Cooking Time: 15 Minutes

Ingredients:

- 2 Tablespoon Poppy Seeds
- 1 Tablespoon Dried Minced Onion
- 2 Teaspoon garlic, minced
- 2 Tablespoon Sesame Seeds
- 1 Teaspoon salt
- 8 Ounce Original Crescent Dough
- 1/4 Cup Dijon mustard
- 1 Large egg, beaten

Directions:

1. When ready to cook, start your smoker at 350 degrees F, and preheat with lid closed, 10 to 15 minutes.

2. Mix together poppy seeds, dried minced onion, dried minced garlic, salt and sesame seeds. Set aside.

3. Cut each triangle of crescent roll dough into thirds lengthwise, making 3 small strips from each roll.

4. Brush the dough strips lightly with Dijon mustard. Put the mini hot dogs on 1 end of the dough and roll up.

5. Arrange them, seam side down, on a greased baking pan. Brush with egg wash and sprinkle with seasoning mixture.

6. Bake in smoker until golden brown, about 12 to 15 minutes.

7. Serve with mustard or dipping sauce of your choice. Enjoy!

Simple Cream Cheese Sausage Balls

Servings: 5

Cooking Time: 30 Minutes

Ingredients:

- 1 pound ground hot sausage, uncooked
- 8 ounces cream cheese, softened
- 1 package mini filo dough shells

Directions:

1. Supply your smoker with wood pellets and follow the start-up procedure. Preheat, with the lid closed, to 350°F.

2. In a large bowl, using your hands, thoroughly mix together the sausage and cream cheese until well blended.

3. Place the filo dough shells on a rimmed perforated pizza pan or into a mini muffin tin.

4. Roll the sausage and cheese mixture into 1-inch balls and place into the filo shells.

5. Place the pizza pan or mini muffin tin on the grill, close the lid, and smoke the sausage balls for 30 minutes, or until cooked through and the sausage is no longer pink.

6. Plate and serve warm.

Chicken Wings With Teriyaki Glaze

Servings: 4

Cooking Time: 50 Minutes

Ingredients:

- 16 large chicken wings, about 3lb (1.4kg) total
- 1 to 1½ tbsp toasted sesame oil
- for the glaze
- ½ cup light soy sauce or tamari
- ¼ cup sake or sugar-free dark-colored soda
- ¼ cup light brown sugar or low-carb substitute
- 2 tbsp mirin or 1 tbsp honey
- 1 garlic clove, peeled, minced or grated
- 2 tsp minced fresh ginger
- 1 tsp cornstarch mixed with 1 tbsp distilled water (optional)
- for serving
- 1 tbsp toasted sesame seeds
- 2 scallions, trimmed, white and green parts sliced sharply diagonally

Directions:

1. Supply your smoker with wood pellets and follow the start-up procedure. Preheat the grill, with the lid closed, to 350° F.

2. Place the chicken wings in a large bowl, add the sesame oil, and turn the wings to coat thoroughly.

3. Place the wings on the grate at an angle to the bars. Grill for 20 minutes and then turn. Continue to cook until the wings are nicely browned and the meat is no longer pink at the bone, about 20 minutes more.

4. To make the glaze, in a saucepan on the stovetop over medium-high heat, combine the ingredients and bring the mixture to a boil. Reduce the glaze by 1/3, about 6 to 8 minutes. If you prefer your glaze to be glossy and thick, add the cornstarch and water mixture to the glaze and cook until it coats the back of a spoon, about 1 to 2 minutes more.

5. Transfer the wings to an aluminum foil roasting pan. Pour the glaze over them, turning to coat thoroughly. Place the pan on the grate and cook the wings until the glaze sets, about 5 to 10 minutes.

6. Transfer the wings to a platter. Scatter the sesame seeds and scallions over the top. Serve with plenty of napkins.

Cold-smoked Cheese

Ingredients:

- 2lb (1kg) well-chilled hard or semi-hard cheese, such as:
- Edam
- Gouda
- Cheddar
- Monterey Jack
- pepper Jack
- goat cheese
- fresh mozzarella
- Muenster
- aged Parmigiano-Reggiano
- Gruyère
- blue cheese

Directions:

1. Unwrap the cheese and remove any protective wax or coating. Cut into 4-ounce (110g) portions to increase the surface area.

2. If possible, move your smoker to a shady area. Place 1 resealable plastic bag filled with ice on top of the drip pan. This is especially important on a warm day because you want to keep the interior temperature of the grill between 70 and 90°F (21 and 32°C) or below.

3. Place a grill mat on one side of the grate. Place the cheese on the mat and allow space between each piece.

4. Fill your smoking tube or pellet maze (see Cast Iron Skillets and Grill Pans) with pellets or sawdust and light according to the manufacturer's instructions. Place the smoking tube on the grate near—but not on—the grill mat. When the tube is smoking consistently, close the grill lid.

5. Smoke the cheese for 1 to 3 hours, replacing the pellets or sawdust and ice if necessary. Monitor the temperature and make sure the cheese isn't beginning to melt. Carefully lift the mat with the cheese to a rimmed baking sheet and let the cheese cool completely before handling.

6. Package the smoked cheese in cheese storage paper or bags or vacuum-seal the cheese, labeling each. (While you can wrap the cheese tightly in plastic wrap, the cheese will spoil faster.) Let the cheese rest for at least 2 to 3 days before eating. It will be even better after 2 weeks.

Bacon-wrapped Jalapeño Poppers

Servings: 12

Cooking Time: 30 Minutes

Ingredients:

- 8 ounces cream cheese, softened
- ½ cup shredded Cheddar cheese
- ¼ cup chopped scallions
- 1 teaspoon chipotle chile powder or regular chili powder
- 1 teaspoon garlic powder
- 1 teaspoon salt
- 18 large jalapeño peppers, stemmed, seeded, and halved lengthwise
- 1 pound bacon (precooked works well)

Directions:

1. Supply your smoker with wood pellets and follow the start-up procedure. Preheat, with the lid closed, to 350°F. Line a baking sheet with aluminum foil.

2. In a small bowl, combine the cream cheese, Cheddar cheese, scallions, chipotle powder, garlic powder, and salt.

3. Stuff the jalapeño halves with the cheese mixture.

4. Cut the bacon into pieces big enough to wrap around the stuffed pepper halves.

5. Wrap the bacon around the peppers and place on the prepared baking sheet.

6. Put the baking sheet on the grill grate, close the lid, and smoke the peppers for 30 minutes, or until the cheese is melted and the bacon is cooked through and crisp.

7. Let the jalapeño poppers cool for 3 to 5 minutes. Serve warm.

Sriracha & Maple Cashews

Servings: 10

Cooking Time: 60 Minutes

Ingredients:

- 2 tbsp unsalted butter
- 3 tbsp pure maple syrup
- 1 tbsp sriracha
- 1 tsp coarse salt (use only if nuts are unsalted)
- 2½ cups unsalted cashews

Directions:

1. Supply your smoker with wood pellets and follow the start-up procedure. Preheat the grill, with the lid closed, to 250° F.

2. In a small saucepan on the stovetop over low heat, melt the butter. Add the maple syrup, sriracha, and salt (if using). Stir until combined. Add the nuts and stir gently to coat thoroughly.

3. Spread the nuts in a single layer in an aluminum foil roasting pan coated with cooking spray. Place the pan on the grate and smoke the nuts until they're lightly toasted, about 1 hour, stirring once or twice.

4. Remove the pan from the grill and let the nuts cool for 15 minutes. They'll be sticky at first but will crisp up. Break them up with your fingers and store at room temperature in an airtight container, such as a lidded glass jar.

BEEF LAMB AND GAME RECIPES

Lamb Chopswith Lemon Vinaigrette

Servings: 4   Cooking Time: 16 Minutes

Ingredients:

- 8 lamb rib chops, about 2lb (1kg) total and each about ¾ inch (2cm) thick
- 3 tbsp extra virgin olive oil
- coarse salt
- freshly ground black pepper
- for the vinaigrette
- 4 lemons, halved
- 1 tbsp plus 1 cup extra virgin olive oil, plus more
- 4 large basil leaves, coarsely chopped
- 1 garlic clove, peeled and coarsely chopped
- 1 tsp Dijon mustard
- 1 tsp honey
- 1 tsp coarse salt
- ½ tsp freshly ground black pepper, plus more

Directions:

1. Supply your smoker with wood pellets and follow the start-up procedure. Preheat the grill, with the lid closed, to 450° F.

2. Coat the lamb chops on each side with the olive oil. Season with salt and pepper. (For the best crust, do this 45 minutes before grilling.)

3. Begin making the vinaigrette by brushing the lemon halves with 1 tablespoon of olive oil. Place the halves cut sides down on the grate and grill until they exhibit some charring, about 6 to 8 minutes. Transfer the lemons to a bowl and let cool.

4. Juice 4 lemon halves through a strainer positioned over a blender. (Reserve the remaining lemon halves for garnishing.) Add the basil leaves, garlic, mustard, honey, and salt and pepper to the blender. Add ¼ cup of olive oil and blend until the garlic is minced and everything's well combined. While the machine's running, slowly add the remaining ¾ cup of olive oil. Taste for seasoning, adding more salt. (If the dressing is too tart, add a little more honey or olive oil—the latter 1 tablespoon at a time.) Transfer the vinaigrette to a pitcher or a cruet.

5. Place the lamb chops on the still-hot grate at an angle to the bars. Grill until the chops have grill marks and the internal temperature reaches 125 to 135°F (52 to 57°C), about 3 to 4 minutes per side.

6. Transfer the chops to a platter and let rest for 3 minutes. Drizzle the lemon vinaigrette over the top. Place 1 reserved lemon half on each plate before serving.

Flavour Texas Twinkies

Servings: 7-14

Cooking Time: 40 Minutes

Ingredients:

➢ 14, slices bacon

➢ ½ cup BBQ sauce

➢ 1 lb. brisket

➢ 8 oz. cream cheese

➢ 1 tsp cumin

➢ 14 large jalapeños

➢ ½ tsp pepper

➢ 1 cup pepper jack cheese, grated

➢ 2 tsp hickory bacon rub

➢ ½ tsp salt

Directions:

1. Supply your smoker with wood pellets and follow the start-up procedure. Preheat the grill, with the lid closed, to 400° F. If using a gas or charcoal grill, set it for medium-high heat.

2. In a food processor, combine the brisket, Hickory Bacon, cumin, salt, pepper, pepper jack and cream cheese. Pulse several times until well combined. Transfer to a bowl and place into refrigerator to chill while preparing jalapeños.

3. Place jalapeños on a sheet tray. Cut each in half lengthwise and remove the seeds and rib with a spoon or by hand, then discard. Note: we recommend using gloves when handling jalapenos, as the seeds can be very hot.

4. Fill each jalapeño half with cream cheese mixture until full, then place other jalapeño half on top. Wrap each jalapeño with a slice of bacon, then skewer crosswise with toothpicks.

5. Place a mesh, metal pan on grill grate and transfer jalapeños to pan. Cover grill and cook for 35 minutes.

6. Open grill and baste jalapeños generously with BBQ sauce, close grill and continue to cook another 5 minutes.

7. Remove from grill and serve hot.

Venison Steaks

Servings: 4

Cooking Time: 80 Minutes

Ingredients:

➢ 4 (8-ounce) venison steaks

➢ 2 tablespoons extra-virgin olive oil

➢ 4 garlic cloves, minced

➢ 1 tablespoon ground sage

➢ 2 teaspoons sea salt

➢ 2 teaspoons freshly ground black pepper

Directions:

1. Supply your smoker with wood pellets and follow the start-up procedure. Preheat, with the lid closed, to 225°F.

2. Rub the venison steaks well with the olive oil and season with the garlic, sage, salt, and pepper.

3. Arrange the venison steaks directly on the grill grate, close the lid, and smoke for 1 hour and 20 minutes, or until a meat thermometer inserted in the center reads 130°F to 140°F, depending on desired doneness. If you want a better sear, remove the steaks from the grill at an internal temperature of 125°F, crank up the heat to 450°F, or the "High" setting, and cook the steaks on each side for an additional 2 to 3 minutes.

Kalbi-style Steak Wraps

<table>
<tr><td>Servings: 4</td><td>Cooking Time: 8 Minutes</td></tr>
</table>

Ingredients:

- 1 flat iron steak, about 1½lb (680g)
- 1 tbsp toasted sesame seeds
- 2 scallions, trimmed, white and green parts thinly sliced on a sharp diagonal
- for the marinade
- 1 small white onion, peeled and coarsely grated
- 4 garlic cloves, peeled and smashed with a chef's knife
- ½ Asian pear, decored and coarsely grated
- ½ cup light soy sauce
- ½ cup low-carb beer or distilled water
- 2 tbsp light brown sugar or low-carb substitute
- 2 tbsp rice vinegar or apple cider vinegar
- 2 tbsp toasted sesame oil
- 1 tbsp peeled and grated fresh ginger
- 1 tsp freshly ground black pepper

Directions:

1. In a large bowl, make the marinade by combining the ingredients. Stir until the sugar dissolves. Place the steaks in a resealable plastic bag and add the marinade, massaging the bag to thoroughly coat the meat. Refrigerate for 8 hours or overnight, turning the bag once or twice.

2. Supply your smoker with wood pellets and follow the start-up procedure. Preheat the grill, with the lid closed, to 450° F.

3. Remove the steaks from the marinade and remove any solids. (Discard the marinade.) Pat dry with paper towels. Place the steaks on the cast iron pan and grill until the internal temperature reaches 125 to 130°F (52 to 54°C), about 3 to 4 minutes per side, turning once.

4. Transfer the steaks to a cutting board and let rest for 2 minutes. Thinly slice each steak on a sharp diagonal and place on a platter. Scatter the sesame seeds and scallions over the top.

5. Place leaf lettuce, thinly sliced jalapeños, fresh cilantro leaves, kimchi (optional), and thinly sliced garlic on a separate platter. Place gochujang (Korean chili paste) in a small ramekin and add that to the platter.

6. Place the two platters on the table. Advise each diner to assemble the lettuce wraps to their desire. Serve with Asian beer, sake, or Korean soju.

Spiced Lamb Burgers With Tzatziki

Servings: 4   Cooking Time: 10 Minutes

Ingredients:

- 1½lb (680g) ground lamb or a mixture of lamb and beef, well chilled
- 1/3 cup grated red onion
- 1 to 2 garlic cloves, peeled and minced
- 2 tbsp chopped fresh dill or fresh mint
- 1 tsp ground cumin
- ½ tsp ground cinnamon
- ½ tsp crushed red pepper flakes (optional)
- extra virgin olive oil
- coarse salt
- freshly ground black pepper

- for the tzatziki
- 1/3 hothouse cucumber, unpeeled and coarsely grated
- coarse salt
- 1½ cups plain Greek yogurt, drained
- 1 to 2 garlic cloves, peeled
- 1 tbsp freshly squeezed lemon juice or white distilled vinegar
- 1½ tbsp extra virgin olive oil
- 1 tbsp chopped fresh dill or fresh mint

Directions:

1. Supply your smoker with wood pellets and follow the start-up procedure. Preheat the grill, with the lid closed, to 450° F.

2. Make the tzatziki by placing the cucumber in a sieve and lightly sprinkle with salt. After 15 minutes, rinse with cold running water. Drain and then squeeze the cucumber dry with paper towels. Transfer the cucumber to a large bowl. Add the yogurt, garlic, and lemon juice. Stir to mix. Season with salt to taste. Transfer to a serving bowl. Set aside. Just before serving, drizzle with the olive oil and scatter the fresh dill over the top.

3. In a large bowl, combine the lamb, red onion, garlic, dill, cumin, cinnamon, and red pepper flakes (if using). Wet your hands with cold water and mix thoroughly but gently. (Try not to overhandle the meat.) Form the meat into 4 patties of equal size, each about ¾ inch (2cm) thick. Use your thumbs to make a shallow depression in the top of each burger. Lightly oil the outsides of the burgers with olive oil. Season with salt and pepper.

4. Place the burgers on the grate and grill until the internal temperature reaches 160°F (71°C), about 4 to 5 minutes per side, turning once.

5. Transfer the burgers to a platter. On a separate platter, place thinly sliced red onions, thinly sliced tomatoes, thinly sliced cucumbers, crumbled feta, and Kalamata olives. Serve with the tzatziki and pita bread.

Grilled Rosemary Rack Of Lamb

Servings: 8

Cooking Time: 30 Minutes

Ingredients:

- 2 Tablespoons Dijon Mustard
- 1 Tablespoon Fresh Parsley, Chopped
- Chop House Steak Rub
- 2 Chine Bones Removed, And Excess Fat Trimmed Racks Of Lamb
- 1 Teaspoon Rosemary, Finely Chopped

Directions:

1. Place the racks of lamb on a flat work surface, then generously brush the lamb all over with Dijon mustard.

2. Season the meat on all sides with Chophouse Steak seasoning and sprinkle with parsley and rosemary.

3. Supply your smoker with wood pellets and follow the start-up procedure. Preheat the grill, with the lid closed, to 400° F.

4. If you're using a gas or charcoal grill, set it up for high heat.

5. Insert a temperature probe into the thickest part of the rack of lamb and sear the rack, meaty side down for about 6 minutes.

6. Remove the lamb from the grill and turn the temperature down to 300°F.

7. Return the lamb to the grill and lean the two racks against each other so that they stand up, and grill for another 20 minutes, or until the internal temperature reaches 130°F.

8. Remove the racks from the grill and allow to rest for 10 minutes before carving and serving.

Smoked Midnight Brisket

Servings: 6

Cooking Time: 720 Minutes

Ingredients:

- 1 Tablespoon Worcestershire sauce
- 1 Tablespoon Beef Rub
- 1 Teaspoon Chicken Rub
- 1 Teaspoon Blackened Saskatchewan Rub
- 1 (4-6 lb) flat cut brisket
- 1 Cup beef broth

Directions:

1. For the Sauce: Whisk Worcestershire sauce and Traeger rubs together in a bowl. Rub mixture into the meat.

2. Supply your smoker with wood pellets and follow the start-up procedure. Preheat the grill, with the lid closed, to 180° F.

3. Place brisket on the grill until internal temperature of the meat reaches 160°F, about 5 to 7 hours. Grill: 180 °F Probe: 160 °F

4. Remove from the grill and double wrap tightly with foil and add 1/2 cup to 1 cup beef broth then return to grill.

5. Increase grill temperature to 225°F and place brisket back on grill 4 to 5 hours until the internal temperature of the meat reaches 204°F. Grill: 225 °F Probe: 204 °F

6. Remove from the grill and let it rest for at least 30 minutes before slicing against the grain. Serve with your favorite Traeger BBQ sauce. Enjoy!

Smoked Spiced Pulled Beef Chuck Roast

Servings: 6-8

Cooking Time: 360 Minutes

Ingredients:

- 1 chuck roast (3-4 pounds)
- 1 yellow or white onion (sliced)
- 3 cups beef stock (divided use)
- SIMPLE BEEF RUB
- 2 Tablespoons kosher salt
- 2 Tablespoons coarse black pepper
- 2 Tablespoons garlic powder

Directions:

1. Supply your smoker with wood pellets and follow the start-up procedure. Preheat the grill, with the lid closed, to 225 °F.

2. Combine all of the ingredients for the rub in a small bowl and rub liberally onto your beef roast, using your hands to press the rub into every surface of the meat.

3. Put the roast directly on your grill grate, fat-side up, and cook for 3 hours. Spray with 1 cup of the beef stock every hour (reserve the other 2 cups of stock).

4. Turn up the heat after 3 hours. Place the sliced onions in the bottom of a large disposable aluminum foil pan and pour the remaining 2 cups of stock in the bottom of the pan. Transfer the roast into the pan on top of the onions and place the pan into the grill.

5. Increase your grill temperature to 250 degrees F, and cook until the internal temperature reaches 165 degrees F (about 3 more hours).

6. Cover the pan tightly with aluminum foil once your roast hits 165 degrees F, and continue cooking until thermometer inserted in the thickest part of the meat reads 200 to 202 degrees F (this step can take another 3 hours). Every roast will be done at a slightly different temperature, so look for your probe to slide into the meat like it is sliding into softened butter.

7. Remove the pan from the smoker and let rest for a few minutes. Separate the roast from the cooking liquid. Shred the roast and separate the fat from the cooking liquid. Moisten the roast with the remaining cooking liquid, or make it into jus for dipping, or turn it into gravy.

Smoked Beef Back Ribs

Servings: 6

Cooking Time: 480 Minutes

Ingredients:

➢ 2 Rack beef back ribs

➢ 1/2 Cup Beef Rub

Directions:

1. If your butcher has not already done so, remove the thin papery membrane from the bone-side of the ribs by working the tip of a butter knife underneath the membrane over a middle bone. Use paper towels to get a firm grip, then tear the membrane off.

2. Season both sides of ribs with Traeger Beef Rub.

3. Supply your smoker with wood pellets and follow the start-up procedure. Preheat the grill, with the lid closed, to 225° F.

4. Arrange the ribs on the grill grate, bone side down. Cook for 8-10 hours, or until internal temperature reaches 205°F . Grill: 225 °F Probe: 205 °F

5. Remove ribs from grill and let rest, lightly covered for 20 minutes before slicing and serving. Enjoy!

Smoked Beef Ribs

Servings: 4-8

Cooking Time: 360 Minutes

Ingredients:

- ➤ 2 (2- or 3-pound) racks beef ribs
- ➤ 2 tablespoons yellow mustard
- ➤ 1 batch Sweet and Spicy Cinnamon Rub

Directions:

1. Supply your smoker with wood pellets and follow the start-up procedure. Preheat the grill, with the lid closed, to 225°F.

2. Remove the membrane from the backside of the ribs. This can be done by cutting just through the membrane in an X pattern and working a paper towel between the membrane and the ribs to pull it off.

3. Coat the ribs all over with mustard and season them with the rub. Using your hands, work the rub into the meat.

4. Place the ribs directly on the grill grate and smoke until their internal temperature reaches between 190°F and 200°F.

5. Remove the racks from the grill and cut them into individual ribs. Serve immediately.

Salt & Pepper Dinosaur Bones

Servings: 3-4

Cooking Time: 480 Minutes

Ingredients:

➢ 1 rack of beef plate short ribs, about 4 to 5lb (1.8 to 2.3kg) total, or 3 bones

➢ coarse kosher salt

➢ freshly ground black pepper

➢ granulated garlic

➢ crushed red pepper flakes (optional)

➢ 1½ cups sugar-free dark-colored soda, sugar-free root beer, beef broth, or brewed coffee

Directions:

1. Supply your smoker with wood pellets and follow the start-up procedure. Preheat the grill, with the lid closed, to 250° F.

2. Place the ribs in an aluminum foil roasting pan. If the rack has a thick cap of fat on the meaty side, trim most of it off because that will impede the formation of a nice bark on the ribs.

3. Generously season the ribs on all sides with salt, pepper, garlic, and red pepper flakes (if using). Place the ribs bone side down on the grate and smoke for 3 hours.

4. Add the soda to a spray bottle and spritz the ribs. Continue to smoke the ribs until the internal temperature reaches 203°F (95°C), about 4 to 5 hours more, spritzing once an hour. (Insert the probe next to the middle rib, being careful not to touch the bone.) When the ribs are tender, the meat will feel gelatinous and springy and will have shrunk back from the ends of the bones by up to 2 inches (5cm).

5. Transfer the ribs to a clean sheet pan and wrap with heavy-duty aluminum foil. Let rest for 1 hour, preferably in an insulated cooler.

6. Slice the ribs apart or remove the meat from the bones and thinly slice before serving with additional salt and pepper.

Smoked Brisket

Servings: 8

Cooking Time: 720 Minutes

Ingredients:

- 2 Tablespoon garlic powder
- 2 Tablespoon onion powder
- 2 Tablespoon paprika
- 2 Teaspoon chile powder
- 1/3 Cup Jacobsen Salt or kosher salt
- 1/3 Cup coarse ground black pepper, divided
- 1 (12-14 lb) whole packer brisket, trimmed
- 1 1/2 Cup beef broth

Directions:

1. Supply your smoker with wood pellets and follow the start-up procedure. Preheat the grill, with the lid closed, to 225° F.

2. For the Rub: Mix together garlic powder, onion powder, paprika, chili pepper, kosher salt and pepper in a small bowl.

3. Season the brisket on all sides with the rub.

4. Place brisket, fat side down on grill grate. Cook brisket until it reaches an internal temperature of 160°F, about 5 to 6 hours. When brisket reaches internal temperature of 160°F, remove from grill. Probe: 160 °F

5. Double wrap meat in aluminum foil and add the beef broth to the foil packet. Return brisket to grill and cook until it reaches an internal temperature of 204°F, about 3 hours more. Probe: 204 °F

6. Once finished, remove from grill, unwrap from foil and let rest for 15 minutes. Slice against the grain and serve.

Flavour Smoked Chuck Roast

Servings: 6

Cooking Time: 540 Minutes

Ingredients:

- 3 cups beef stock, divided
- 1, 3 lb chuck roast
- 3 tbsp sweet heat rub
- 1 yellow onion

Directions:

1. Place chuck roast in a 9x13 baking pan. Sprinkle generously with Sweet Heat Rub and rub to coat evenly on all sides.

2. Cover pan with foil and refrigerate overnight.

3. The next day, remove chuck roast from refrigerator and let it come to room temperature.

4. Supply your smoker with wood pellets and follow the start-up procedure. Preheat the grill, with the lid closed, to 225° F. If using a gas or charcoal grill, set it for low heat.

5. Insert a temperature probe into the thickest side of the roast, then place chuck roast directly on grill grate. Close lid and smoke for 3 hours.

6. Spray roast with 1 cup of beef stock every hour.

7. Slice the onion and place in a 9x13 aluminum pan. Pour the remaining cup of stock over the onions and set roast on top of onions.

8. Increase temperature to 250°F and cook an additional 2 ½ to 3 hours, or until internal temperature reaches 165°F.

9. Once 165°F internal temperature is reached, cover roast with aluminum foil, and cook another 2 ½ to 3 hours, or until internal temperature reaches 200°F.

10. Remove chuck roast from grill.

11. Allow roast to rest 15 minutes, then remove from pan and shred with meat claws. For added moistness and flavor, pour some remaining cooking stock over the shredded roast and serve.

COCKTAILS RECIPES

Bacon Old-fashioned Cocktail

Servings: 2

Cooking Time: 20 Minutes

Ingredients:

- 16 Slices bacon
- 1/2 Cup warm water (110°F to 115°F)
- 1500 mL bourbon
- 1/2 Fluid Ounce maple syrup
- 4 Dash Angostura bitters
- 2 fresh orange peel

Directions:

1. Smoke bacon prior to making Old Fashioned using this recipe for Applewood Smoked Bacon.

2. To Make Bacon: Supply your smoker with wood pellets and follow the start-up procedure. Preheat the grill, with the lid closed, to 325° F.

3. Place bacon in a single layer on a cooling rack that fits inside a baking sheet pan. Cook in Traeger for 15-20 minutes or until bacon is browned and crispy. Reserve bacon for later. Let the fat cool slightly; you'll use the fat to infuse the bourbon. Grill: 325 °F

4. Combine 1/4 cup of warm (not hot) liquid bacon fat with the entire contents of a 750ml bottle of bourbon in a glass or heavy plastic container.

5. Use a fork to stir well. Let it sit on the counter for a few hours, stirring every so often.

6. After about four hours, put bourbon fat mixture into the freezer. After about an hour, the fat will congeal and you can simply scoop it out with a spoon. You can fine-strain the mixture through a sieve to remove all fat if desired.

7. Combine ingredients with ice and stir until cold. Strain over fresh ice in an Old Fashioned glass and garnish with reserved bacon and orange peel. Enjoy!

Traeger Old Fashioned

Servings: 2

Cooking Time: 60 Minutes

Ingredients:

- ➢ 2 orange
- ➢ 2 Cup cherries
- ➢ 3 Ounce bourbon
- ➢ 1 Ounce Smoked Simple Syrup
- ➢ 8 Dash Bitters Lab Apricot Vanilla Bitters

Directions:

1. Supply your smoker with wood pellets and follow the start-up procedure. Preheat the grill, with the lid closed, to 180° F.

2. While Traeger preheats, slice whole orange into wheels.

3. Place cherries on a small sheet pan and place in the Traeger. Place orange slices directly on the grill grate.

4. Smoke cherries for 1 hour and oranges for 25 minutes, depending on taste, before removing from the grill. Let oranges and cherries cool. Grill: 180 °F

5. Pour bourbon into glass, followed by Traeger Smoked Simple Syrup and bitters. Add ice and stir for 45 seconds or until drink is well-diluted.

6. Strain contents into new glass over fresh ice. Skewer orange wheel and add cherry for garnish. Enjoy!

Smoked Barnburner Cocktail

Servings: 2

Cooking Time: 45 Minutes

Ingredients:

- 16 Ounce fresh raspberries
- 1/2 Cup Smoked Simple Syrup
- 1 1/2 Ounce smoked raspberry syrup
- 3 Ounce reposado tequila
- 1 Ounce lime juice
- 1 Ounce lemon juice
- 2 grilled lime wheel, for garnish

Directions:

1. Supply your smoker with wood pellets and follow the start-up procedure. Preheat the grill, with the lid closed, to 180° F.

2. For Smoked Raspberry Syrup: Place fresh raspberries on a grill mat and smoke for 30 minutes. After the raspberries have been smoked, reserve a few for garnish and place the remainder into a shallow sheet pan with Traeger Smoked Simple Syrup. Grill: 180 °F

3. Place sheet pan on the grill grate and smoke for 45 minutes. Remove from grill and let cool. Strain through a fine mesh sieve discarding solids. Transfer the syrup to the refrigerator until ready to use. Makes about 1/2 cup of smoked raspberry syrup. Grill: 180 °F

4. For cocktail: Add 3/4 ounce smoked raspberry syrup, tequila, lime juice and lemon juice with ice into a mixing glass. Shake and pour over clean ice. Garnish with smoked raspberries and a grilled lime wheel. Enjoy!

Smoked Pumpkin Spice Latte

Servings: 4

Cooking Time: 45 Minutes

Ingredients:

- 1 Small sugar pumpkin
- olive oil
- 1 Can sweetened condensed milk
- 1 Cup whole milk
- 2 Tablespoon Smoked Simple Syrup
- 1 Teaspoon pumpkin pie spice
- pinch of salt
- cinnamon
- whipped cream
- shaved nutmeg
- 8 Ounce smoked cold brew coffee

Directions:

1. Supply your smoker with wood pellets and follow the start-up procedure. Preheat the grill, with the lid closed, to 325° F.

2. Cut the sugar pumpkin in half, scoop out the seeds and discard. Place the pumpkin halves cut side up on a baking sheet and brush lightly with olive oil.

3. Place the sheet tray directly on the grill grate and cook 45 minutes or until the flesh is tender. Remove from heat and place on the counter to cool. Grill: 325 °F

4. When the pumpkin is cool enough to handle, scoop out the flesh and mash until smooth.

5. Place 3 Tbsp of the pumpkin puree in a separate bowl and reserve the remaining for another use.

6. Add the sweetened condensed milk, whole milk, Traeger Smoked Simple Syrup, pumpkin pie seasoning and salt to the pumpkin puree. Whisk to combine.

7. Pour the cold brew over ice, add desired amount of pumpkin spice creamer and top with whipped cream, cinnamon, and shaved nutmeg if desired. Enjoy!

Smoked Plum And Thyme Fizz Cocktail

Servings: 2

Cooking Time: 60 Minutes

Ingredients:

- 6 fresh plums
- 4 Fluid Ounce vodka
- 1 1/2 Fluid Ounce fresh lemon juice
- 2 Ounce smoked plum and thyme simple syrup
- 4 Fluid Ounce club soda
- 2 Slices smoked plum, for garnish
- 2 Sprig fresh thyme, for garnish
- 8 Sprig thyme
- 2 Cup Smoked Simple Syrup

Directions:

1. Supply your smoker with wood pellets and follow the start-up procedure. Preheat the grill, with the lid closed, to 180° F.

2. Cut plums in half and remove the pit. Place the plum halves directly on the grill grate and smoke for 25 minutes. Grill: 180 ˚F

3. For the Plum and Thyme Simple Syrup: After 25 minutes, remove plums from the grill and cut into quarters. Add plums and thyme sprigs to 1 cup of Traeger Smoked Simple Syrup. Smoke the mixture for 45 minutes. Remove from grill, strain and let cool. Grill: 180 ˚F

4. Add vodka, fresh lemon juice and smoked plum and thyme simple syrup to a mixing glass.

5. Add ice and shake. Strain over clean ice, top off with club soda and garnish with a piece of thyme and slice of smoked plum. Enjoy!

Grilled Peach Sour Cocktail

Servings: 2

Cooking Time: 15 Minutes

Ingredients:

- 2 peach, sliced
- 2 Tablespoon sugar
- 1 1/2 Ounce Smoked Simple Syrup
- 4 Ounce bourbon
- 6 Dash Bitters Lab Apricot Vanilla Bitters
- 2 Sprig fresh thyme, for garnish

Directions:

1. Supply your smoker with wood pellets and follow the start-up procedure. Preheat the grill, with the lid closed, to 325° F.

2. Toss peach slices with granulated sugar and place directly on grill grate. Cook for 20 minutes or until grill marks form. Remove from grill and let cool. Grill: 325 ˚F

3. Place peaches and Traeger Smoked Simple Syrup into tin and muddle. Peaches should form about an ounce of juice during the muddling. Once completed, add remaining ingredients and shake.

4. Pour contents into glass over fresh ice and garnish with fresh thyme. Enjoy!

Ryes And Shine Cocktail

Servings: 2

Cooking Time: 30 Minutes

Ingredients:

- 2 lemon, cut into wheels for garnish
- 6 Tablespoon granulated sugar
- 2 Ounce rye
- 1 Ounce bourbon
- 3 Ounce lemon juice
- 1 Ounce Smoked Simple Syrup
- 6 Dash Fernet-Branca

Directions:

1. Supply your smoker with wood pellets and follow the start-up procedure. Preheat the grill, with the lid closed, to 325° F.

2. Toss lemon wheels with granulated sugar to coat on both sides. Place wheels directly on the grill grate and cook for 15 minutes on each side or until grill marks form. Grill: 325 ˚F

3. Add rye, bourbon, lemon juice, Traeger Smoked Simple Syrup and Fernet-Branca to a shaker and shake until slightly diluted (about 10 to 15 seconds).

4. Pour into a fresh glass, serve neat and garnish with a grilled lemon wheel. Enjoy!

Smoked Sangria

Servings: 6

Cooking Time: 45 Minutes

Ingredients:

- ➢ 1 (750 ml) medium-bodied red wine
- ➢ 1/4 Cup Grand Marnier
- ➢ 1/4 Cup Smoked Simple Syrup
- ➢ 1 Cup fresh cranberries
- ➢ 1 Whole apple, sliced
- ➢ 2 Whole limes, sliced
- ➢ 4 cinnamon stick
- ➢ soda water

Directions:

1. Supply your smoker with wood pellets and follow the start-up procedure. Preheat the grill, with the lid closed, to 180° F.

2. In a shallow dish, combine red wine, Grand Marnier, Traeger Smoked Simple Syrup and cranberries, and place directly on the grill grate.

3. Smoke for 30 to 45 minutes or until the liquid picks up desired amount of smoke. Remove from grill and place in the fridge to cool. Grill: 180 ˚F

4. When the mixture has cooled, place in a large pitcher. Add sliced apples, limes, cinnamon sticks and ice to pitcher.

5. Top with soda water, if desired. Enjoy!

Smoky Mountain Bramble Cocktail

Servings: 2

Cooking Time: 15 Minutes

Ingredients:

➢ 16 Ounce blackberries

➢ 2 Cup sugar

➢ 10 smoked blackberries

➢ 3 Ounce vodka

➢ 1 1/2 Ounce Alpine Distilling Preserve Liqueur

➢ 1 1/2 Ounce lemon juice

➢ 1 Ounce smoked blackberry syrup

Directions:

1. Supply your smoker with wood pellets and follow the start-up procedure. Preheat the grill, with the lid closed, to 180° F.

2. To make Smoked Blackberry Simple Syrup: Place blackberries on a grill mat and smoke for 15 to 20 minutes. Grill: 180 °F

3. Combine 1 cup water and sugar in a small sauce pan and warm over medium heat until sugar dissolves. Remove from heat and place 2/3 of blackberries in the simple syrup and macerate.

4. Strain through a fine mesh strainer and store for up to 14 days.

5. To make the cocktail: Muddle 4 to 5 smoked blackberries in a cocktail shaker. Add vodka, Preserve Liqueur, lemon and smoked blackberry syrup. Add ice and shake vigorously. Double strain into an old fashioned glass.

6. Garnish with a smoked blackberry and lemon twist. Enjoy!

Grilled Peach Mint Julep

Servings: 2

Cooking Time: 45 Minutes

Ingredients:

- 2 Whole peach
- 4 Ounce whiskey
- 2 Cup sugar
- 4 Tablespoon pink peppercorns
- 20 Whole fresh mint leaves, plus more for garnish
- 2 lime wedge, for garnish
- 4 Ounce bourbon

Directions:

1. For the Grilled Whiskey Peaches: cut peach into slices, then soak peach slices in whiskey in the refrigerator for 4 to 6 hours.

2. For the Pink Peppercorn Simple Syrup: In a shallow pan, combine sugar, 1 cup water and pink peppercorns.

3. Supply your smoker with wood pellets and follow the start-up procedure. Preheat the grill, with the lid closed, to 180° F.

4. Cook syrup down on the grill for 30 minutes, or until desired smoke flavor has been reached. Remove from the grill. Grill: 180 °F

5. Increase Traeger temperature to 350°F and preheat. Place the whiskey peach slices directly on the grill grate and cook 10 to 12 minutes or until peaches soften and get grill marks. Grill: 350 °F

6. To make the Julep: Muddle 1/2 ounce Pink Peppercorn Simple Syrup with 10 fresh mint leaves and 4 slices of grilled whiskey peaches.

7. Add crushed ice over the rim of the glass. Pour bourbon over the crushed ice and stir. Garnish with 1 large sprig of mint and fresh lime. Enjoy!

Batter Up Cocktail

Servings: 2

Cooking Time: 60 Minutes

Ingredients:

- ➢ 2 whole nutmeg
- ➢ 4 Ounce Michter's Bourbon
- ➢ 3 Teaspoon pumpkin puree
- ➢ 1 Ounce Smoked Simple Syrup
- ➢ 2 Large egg

Directions:

1. Supply your smoker with wood pellets and follow the start-up procedure. Preheat the grill, with the lid closed, to 180° F.

2. Place whole nutmeg on a sheet tray and place in the grill. Smoke 1 hour. Remove from grill and let cool. Grill: 180 ˚F

3. Add everything to a shaker and shake without ice. Add ice, then shake and strain into a chilled highball glass.

4. Garnish with grated, smoked nutmeg. Enjoy!